Devotions to Build Up Your Relationships

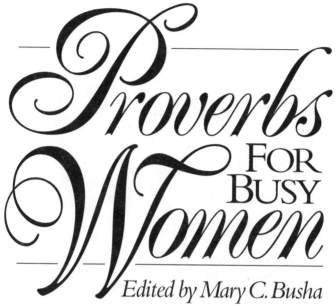

Proverbs
FOR
BUSY
Women

Edited by Mary C. Busha

Contributors include Ruth Bell Graham,
Beverly LaHaye, and Annie Chapman

BROADMAN
&HOLMAN
PUBLISHERS

Nashville, Tennessee

4253-87
0-8054-5387-3

Dewey Decimal Classification: 242.643
Subject Heading: Devotional Literature \ Woman—Religious Life \
Bible. O.T. Proverbs
Library of Congress Card Catalog Number: 94-36448

Scripture passages marked AMP are from The Amplified Bible, Old Testament copyright © 1962, 1964 by Zondervan Publishing House, used by permission, and the New Testament © The Lockman Foundation 1954, 1958, 1987, used by permission; KJV, the King James Version; NAB, the New American Bible, © 1970 Confraternity of Christian Doctrine, Washington, D.C., published by P.J. Kennedy & Sons, New York; NASB, the New American Standard Bible, © the Lockman Foundation, 1960, 1962, 1963, 1968, 1971, 1972, 1973, 1975, 1977, used by permission; NIV, the Holy Bible, New International Version, copyright © 1973, 1978, 1984 by International Bible Society; NKJV, the New King James Version, copyright © 1979, 1980, 1982, Thomas Nelson, Inc., Publishers; RSV, the Revised Standard Version of the Bible, copyrighted 1946, 1952, © 1971, 1973; and TLB, The Living Bible, copyright © Tyndale House Publishers, Wheaton, Ill., 1971, used by permission.

Interior design by Leslie Joslin
Cover design by The Puckett Group

Library of Congress Cataloging-in-Publication Data
Proverbs for today's women / Mary Busha, editor
    p. cm.
Contents: 1. Devotions to refresh you in your work — 2. Devotions to build up your relationships — 3. Devotions to strengthen your walk with God.
ISBN 0-8054-5387-3
1. Bible. O.T. Proverbs—Meditations. 2. Women—Prayer-books and devotions—English. 3. Christian life. I. Bushā, Mary Catherine, 1945–.
  BS1465.4.P76   1995
  242'.643—dc20
                                       94-36448
                                         CIP

*This book in the series
is dedicated
to
R.W.B.
my greatest supporter,
my best friend.*

*With all my love,
M.C.B.*

Acknowledgments

Mary C. Busha

In compiling a book about relationships, it would be difficult not to mention literally hundreds of people who deserve appreciation. Those who contributed to the writings for the devotional series, those who upheld us all with their prayers, many, many thanks!

Special appreciation goes to our editor Janis Whipple and to Broadman and Holman Publishers. Thank you for allowing this dream to continue.

And to my husband, Bob, for his ever-present smile and words of encouragement. You are my greatest supporter; I appreciate you more than words can express.

CONTENTS

INTRODUCTION

"No man is an island entire of itself," said John Donne a few hundred years ago. How true his words are, especially in Christianity. Relationship is of prime concern to God. If it were not so, He would have left Adam alone on this earth. If it were not so, He would not have sent His Son into the world to seek and to save the lost.

Contained within the pages of this book are examples of people interacting with people—of relationships. In some cases, it is a mutual interaction with near equal give-and-take on the parts of all concerned. In other cases, it is how others have influenced and ministered in the lives of those who have shared their lives in their writings. In still other instances, it is how the writers have been used to influence another's life.

God did not create us to live alone. And through His Word He set forth principles for us to learn and put into practice in order to get along with others.

"Any man's death diminishes me, because I am involved in mankind," Donne continues. And so it is with you and me. We are involved in mankind. May this book be a source of encouragement in your relationships and in your involvement with those around you.

No Longer Homeless

DeLaine Anderson

Speak up and judge fairly;
defend the rights of the poor and needy.
Proverbs 31:9

"You want to bring home whom?" I asked. Andrea, our college sophomore, wanted permission to bring home a homeless friend, twenty-three years her senior, for Thanksgiving.

"And could he stay overnight?" she pleaded. "He has no place to go."

Oh, oh, I thought, *it's practice-what-you-preach time.* But was it safe to allow him to come? And stay overnight? How would our other guests react? Feeling quite uneasy, I consented.

As we shared dinner on Thanksgiving Day, Bruce related anecdotes of a life foreign to us. That night he slept in a sleeping bag on the floor rather than in the guest room. "I wouldn't know what to do with white sheets," he quipped with a toothless grin.

Early next morning as the family slept, Bruce and I sat at the kitchen table. Breakfast included an animated documentary about the dangers and frustrations of street living. A smooth transition to spiritual matters occurred when Bruce related a close-call automobile accident.

"Bruce," I queried, "If you had died in that accident, do you know for certain that you would have gone to heaven?" He thought that he would have. "How can you be so sure?" I probed.

"I've got sins," Bruce said with a penetrating gaze. "But when I get to the gate, I'll tell the guard he has to let me in because Jesus Christ is my lawyer." Way to go, Bruce!

The apostle John wrote likewise in 1 John 2:1, "But if anybody does sin, we have one who speaks to the Father in our defense—Jesus Christ, the Righteous One." Bruce's advocate. His defender.

Bruce is no longer homeless. He died, partially due to improperly healed wounds sustained in a street fight. We grieved at the loss of our daughter's friend. But Bruce has another Friend who understands him perfectly. His Lawyer, Jesus Christ, met him at the heavenly threshold and signaled the gatekeeper to open wide the gate. Arm in arm, the Defender and defended one passed through.

Father, as Jesus my Advocate and Defender
pleads my case in the heavenly court, may I
speak up for and defend the rights of the poor
and needy in the world around us.
Amen.

THANKS FOR TALKING TO ME

Delores Elaine Bius

Heaviness in the heart of man maketh it stoop:
but a good word maketh it glad.
Proverbs 12:25, KJV

With a smile rivaling that of the toothiest jack-o-lantern, the elderly gentleman in the motorized cart said, "Thanks for talking to me," after our short conversation on the sidewalk near our homes.

My few words had obviously brightened up his day and been a respite in an otherwise boring and restricted life. Yet that conversation had taken only a few moments out of my day.

Only the week before I had met a teacher at my grand-daughter's high school who had spoken those same words. Recognizing him as having taught history to my own sons a decade earlier, I rushed over to greet him. Not yet of retirement age, he had obviously suffered a stroke that had left him unable to speak very well.

My granddaughter later told me that some of his students made fun of him behind his back. Even some adults avoided talking with him, she said, because it was a slow process for him to get his words out. Yet he was still a good teacher.

I reminded him of my sons and remarked that I was at the school for my granddaughter's appearance in a school play. He was interested in hearing how my sons were progressing in their jobs. Then, when I was leaving him, he said, "Thanks for talking to me." His comment left me with a warm feeling inside.

Both of these incidents made me resolve to spend more of my time talking to the lonely people I come across. There are so many, too, from the little neighbor boy whose parents both work and have little time to answer his many questions, to the elderly widow who has outlived most of her friends and whose few relatives live faraway.

A few minutes out of my schedule is a small price to pay for bringing a ray of sunshine into someone's life. Those words, "Thanks for talking to me," are a greater payment than diamonds or gold!

Thank You, Father, for reminding me
that my words can gladden the hearts of
those around me.
Amen.

NO STRANGER TO HIM

Myra Boone

The fruit of righteousness is a tree of life,
and he who is wise wins souls.
Proverbs 11:30, NASB

Leaning against the water machine outside the grocery store, I overheard one white-haired man say to another, while filling a plastic bottle with drinking water, "Yeah, they didn't think I was going to make it. Doctors almost lost me."

I studied the old gentleman as he described his failing body; his faded, baggy pants were held up by a brown belt cinched tightly around his waist, camouflaging his thin, weakened condition. A familiar urging broke my concentration. "Soon this man could be standing before Me. Wouldn't you like to tell him how he could spend eternity in heaven?"

I knew the Spirit's prompting well. "But, Lord!" I responded. "What . . . how? I don't even know this man!"

"I do," He gently reminded me. "Just let Me give you the words."

As quickly as my heart nodded in agreement, I heard what seemed like the most feeble sentence I'd ever spoken emerge from my mouth: "I'm sure glad the Lord gives us 'living water'—the kind that really satisfies."

"I'm satisfied!" the white-haired man announced with a smile, turning to look at me.

"Oh, do you know Jesus?" I retorted.

"Not personally. Do you?"

"Yes, as a matter of fact, I do!"

"Well, tell me all about it," he spoke with warm sincerity.

As I muttered nervously, his eyes were fixed intently on mine. Soon the questions he asked were penetrating my fear, taking me to the invisible realities. The Lord kept His word; He filled my mouth with truth. The gospel clearly unfolded in a few short minutes.

The man stood speechless as I continued. His face, though marked with age, looked curiously childlike. As we parted, he shook my hand, thanking me and promising to think seriously about what we had discussed. I grinned, sensing the pleasure of the One who loved the white-haired man more than I. Deep peace filled my heart, knowing this man had heard how heaven could be his.

Father, thanks for sharing Your heart with me
and for allowing me to be Your mouthpiece to
a troubled world. Make me willing to love
people enough to tell them about You.
Amen.

A HUG FOR
THE ROAD

Catherine Brandt

*An anxious heart weighs a man down,
but a kind word cheers him up.*
Proverbs 12:25

Jodi's ambition was to drive to Alaska before ice and blizzards made the roads impassable. Halfway to her destination, in the wilds of Canada, the storm made her stop to survey the situation.

She pulled into a truck stop for a hot meal. Two tractor trailers stood outside. *Maybe I can get some encouragement from the drivers*, she thought.

The two drivers were the only other customers. "Might as well share our table," the man with a beard said.

Jodi sat down and ordered.

"Where you headed?" asked the other man.

"Fairbanks," Jodi said. "My brother and sister-in-law live up there."

"In that beat-up car?" the bearded driver asked.

"Well, I'm going to try," Jodi said. After listening to their tales of Alaskan blizzards and ten-foot-deep snow drifts, she began to wonder if she should quit.

Their meals finished, the other driver said, "Come along, and we'll hug you."

Jodi jumped up from her place. "No way!"

"Not that, sister," the driver with the beard said with a chuckle. "Jack will start out first, then your little car, then I'll back you up. We'll hug you all the way."

Many times when I've been bewildered by life's storms and ready to quit, God has provided an encourager—a hug for the road. An encourager is someone who will lead you over rough roads, someone who will back you up, and someone who, with kind words, will cheer you on.

"Come on. You can do it. Let me show you how. Just follow me."

Because our loving heavenly Father has provided encouragers for me, I take it He wants me to be one too.

I don't have to go far to find a discouraged person in need of cheering. The world is crowded with discouraged people, ready to quit, weighed down with anxiety, needing a kind word to cheer them—needing a hug for the road.

Dear Lord, make me aware of those in my life

today who need encouragement and kind

words to cheer them on.

Amen.

MOLLY
MOP TOP

Georgia E. Burkett

A joyful heart makes a cheerful face,
but when the heart is sad, the spirit is broken.
Proverbs 15:13, NASB

I've always envied clowns. Their white faces and exaggerated grins always seemed to hide a mysterious "other person." How I wished that I, too, could mask the ordinary me and let my imagination take over.

My chance came when I was asked to try clowning for a children's program. So for fun, I decided to portray a cherished favorite from my childhood, Molly Mop Top, an old rag doll.

Something akin to magic happened the moment I covered my face with slick, white grease paint. Widely arched black eyebrows, blue polka-dotted cheeks, and a nonsensical, ear-to-ear red grin all gave my face an expression of rollicking surprise. A fluffy, white mop tied off in pigtails covered my hair, and an expansive white apron broadcast my motto, Jesus Is

My Friend. In the mirror I saw, instead of a little old grandmother, a floppy rag doll.

The children and I had so much fun that I almost wished I could remain Molly Mop Top forever. Then, before I finished, I briefly explained the motto on my apron and told the children how Jesus became my Friend, and how He could become their Friend too.

Within weeks I was asked to clown for residents in a nursing home. Even with modifications to make my performance more suitable to the elderly, the magic worked again. Molly Mop Top frolicked among those weary, time-worn folks like an animated doll.

The despair and resignation so evident on the faces of those dear souls were soon replaced with grins and chuckles. As I drew them into my act with riddles, jokes, and funny songs, they clapped and sang and called for more. I couldn't help but feel that the Lord was looking down, enjoying the fun with us. When I reminded them that my Friend, Jesus, wanted to be their Friend, too, they smiled and said, "Yes, yes, my Friend, too."

Proverbs 15:13 truly says it all. A sad heart can't help but weary the spirit. However, God has given us talents to cheer both young and old. And when we do, our own hearts are gladdened even more than those to whom we minister.

Dear Lord, may I, Your servant,

always delight in sharing with others the

unquenchable spirit of joy that You give me.

Amen.

O AGATHA!

Mary C. Busha

A man has joy in an apt answer,
and how delightful is a timely word!
Proverbs 15:23, NASB

"Friends!" four-year-old Daniel shouted from his front yard, announcing to the children in his new neighborhood that he was now up from his afternoon nap and ready to play. Kids are darling and so uninhibited.

One day, my daughter, Laura, heard Daniel say to one of the little neighbor girls, "O Agatha, our God is an awesome God; He reigns." On another occasion he told little Janene, "Jesus loves us and is watching over us." Still another time, he insisted on bringing home his Sunday School take-home paper and giving it to another neighborhood friend.

I wish I was as uninhibited and unashamed in my neighborhood witnessing as little Daniel is in his. What holds me back from sharing as openly and freely as my little grandson? Could it be fear of offending someone? Fear of being

rejected? Fear of not knowing what to say? I wonder, are Daniel's methods something I could adopt?

Let's see. To Agatha he proclaimed the majesty of our Lord. To Janene he spoke of Jesus' love and concern. And to yet another friend he shared the written word.

Would it be so hard for me to compliment my neighbor's beautiful flower garden and at the same time speak of God's marvelous creation? Would it be so hard for me to go see the lonely widow just two doors down and remind her that there is Someone who loves her and cares about her? And how about my neighbor across the street who just moved in? Perhaps a plate of homemade muffins would welcome her into the neighborhood, and one of the Christian books that's encouraged me lately would touch her too.

Thank you, Daniel. I believe I see a lesson here. I don't have to carry around a tract outlining the four spiritual laws and be ready to pounce on the first person who walks down the street. I just have to go about my normal day with a timely word and an openness to share freely and unashamedly the goodness and glory of my Lord.

Thank You, Father, for Daniel's example. I
look forward to the opportunities You're going
to present in my neighborhood to share freely
and openly Your goodness and Your love.
Amen.

MAN'S PLAN, GOD'S PATH

Barbara Caponegro

A man's mind plans his way,
but the LORD directs his steps.
Proverbs 16:9, RSV

To get beyond the problems of life, sometimes you have to look back and count the number of footsteps it took to get you to where you are now. I did that one day as I waited my turn at the shoe repair shop.

Looking out the window into the unfamiliar street, my mind turned to happier days, days before relocation entered my life. Those years were happy, safe, and predictable.

Pat, my husband, taught school and worked a second job. As the needs of our young family increased, he decided to enter the sales force rather than have me work. It was important for both of us that I stay at home and care for our children. His success and hard work afforded us that desire. Promotions were accepted happily, until one meant a major move.

My life changed dramatically! Gone were familiar faces and places. But the biggest change was the anger I had toward my husband. I prayed to the Lord to release me from these feelings. I needed His wisdom to help me cope and understand my new lifestyle.

I was jolted back to the present as the shoe repairman asked me what needed to be fixed on the shoes. As I showed him the thin soles and worn heels, I realized that Pat had just bought these shoes before we moved here. How many miles did he have to walk to wear them out so soon?

In a split second, I traced the path of Pat's footsteps that brought us this far. The amount of love, dedication, and energy he exerted daily accomplished our plan to keep me home to raise the children. But it was God's direction of Pat's steps that led us here. I finally understood!

I started to weep. The shoe repairman asked me what was wrong.

How do you explain to a stranger that, as I stood standing in line for Pat's heels and soles to be repaired, God repaired my soul?

That evening, my husband was surprised to find me waiting for him at the front door holding his shoes and smiling.

Dear Father, I bow before You,

grateful for the paths we have traveled.

There is security and comfort in knowing

that You direct our steps no matter

what path we may choose.

Amen.

WHOSE FATHER'S DAY?

Irene Carloni

A wise son heeds his father's instruction.
Proverbs 13:1

It was June, the middle of the year. I was in morning prayer when Father's Day popped into my mind. My thoughts escalated to my heavenly Father. I meditated on how wonderful He is. How thankful I am that He chose and predestined me. He sacrificed so much for me. Every day is His Father's day.

Continuing in prayer, the Holy Spirit quickened me to remember my earthly father. He and my mother had come to the United States from middle Europe. They had raised nine children during the years when our country was going through severe economic difficulties.

My father had provided all nine of us with a parochial school education. He was active in the church parish and provided as much financial support to the church as he was able. He instilled in all of us the fear of the Lord and the basics of

Christianity. He taught us to honor the Lord, to give to the poor, and to live honest and moral lives. He passed away in June, thirty-seven years ago.

The Holy Spirit quickened me again and showed me my heavenly Father's wonderful plan: He sent His Son to write the gospel on the hearts of men. My father received this heritage and taught his children a plan for living and serving the Lord. And now the mantle has been passed on to my children with the prayer that their Christian foundation will go on to their children. A warm feeling of comfort enveloped me as I thanked God for my Christian parents who are now in heaven with Him.

> *My Lord, my heavenly Father, I thank You so*
> *much for giving me a Christian earthly father.*
> *Let me not forget to thank You and praise You*
> *for being my heavenly Father forever.*
> *Amen.*

A WORD
FITLY SPOKEN

Julie Carobine

Anxiety in the heart of man causes depression,
but a good word makes it glad.
Proverbs 12:25, NKJV

"Just sign me up!" growled the old man, tossing a $100 bill onto the counter.

I admit I didn't like this customer's gruff attitude. There wasn't much in his voice that made me want to help him. Still, I knew better than to give in to my irritation. After all, I had a job to do.

"Would you like to pay for your membership on a monthly or yearly basis, sir?" I asked, hesitantly.

"I don't care. Just get me started!" he snapped.

I could see he was not going to help me much. Usually I enjoyed working the front counter of our local YMCA. Most members chatted and joked with each visit. Why was this man so negative?

Reluctantly, I decided to take this situation in a different direction. When asking for his address, he mentioned he had just relocated from another state. So while we were both filling out the necessary paperwork, I struck up a conversation with him.

Catching a glimpse of his name from the registration card he was filling out, I asked, "So, Harry, what brought you to Ventura?"

"Oh, my wife died and my kids all moved away."

Aha! As his answer tugged at my heart, I knew why his disposition was not the most cheerful one ever. Suddenly I felt privileged to be in a position to help him. *He needs us,* I thought.

Our conversation became upbeat as I suggested several programs for Harry to take part in, and he became like a young boy in a toy store, fascinated with the opportunities before him. During our short time together, I couldn't help but be elated at the sight of the transformation I was witnessing: the softening of his face, an excitement in his voice.

It felt terrific to help someone and to know that, in my own small way, I was following the Lord's will. Through this I learned that I must be cheerful and giving even during those times when it may not be comfortable to do so.

Harry walked out that day with a smile on his face, and I hope a song on his heart.

Dear Lord, teach me to be the comfort to others

that You are to me. I pray You will give me the

confidence I need to live by Your example.

Amen.

FOR SUCH A TIME AS THIS

Amelia Chaffee

*The light in the eyes [of him whose heart is
joyful] rejoices the heart of others,
and good news nourishes the bones.*
Proverbs 15:30, AMP

"Dear, do you ever pray?" my mother asked me, reaching for my hand across the crumb-littered table.

I considered the question as my eye scanned the unwashed dishes on the counter and the unfolded laundry scattered about the living room.

No, I couldn't say prayer was part of my life. For although I had never doubted God's existence, He seemed distant, unknowable. What did He have to do with coping with toddlers and a house that simply would not stay clean?

I listened as my mother described her recent conversion to Christianity. I was happy for her, for she was obviously at peace with this Jesus she talked about. However, the concept of a personal relationship with God was not one to which I could relate.

That is, until two days later. I was again trying hopelessly to conquer the mess that was my home when the doorbell rang. Standing there was a lovely young woman and her two young children. As we were new to the neighborhood, I was very pleased to see potential playmates for my own moppets.

After we all got acquainted, my neighbor explained she had recently rededicated her life to the Lord and had felt very strongly that someone on the block needed to hear about Him. The conviction was so powerful, she knew she must be obedient to find that person. So she bundled her son into his stroller, took her two-year-old by the hand, and started up the street.

She met with rejection or indifference at house after house, and as she approached the last house—mine—she was beginning to wonder who she was being sent to talk to.

As she explained, I suddenly knew that God was not only real, but that He cared about me, personally.

My mother, who had begged God to send someone I could relate to, cried tears of joy that He had done just that. I asked Jesus to be my Lord and Savior shortly after that visit. And, praise God, although my house is still not perfect, my soul is finally in order.

Oh, Lord, thank You for sending those with
joyful hearts to share the good news with me.
Make me always willing to pass on that joy to
those who hunger for You, that You may
nourish them too.
Amen.

THE BEST
NEWS OF ALL

Susan Childress

Like cold water to a weary soul,
so is good news from a distant land.
Proverbs 25:25, NASB

Sixteen years ago, my husband and I packed all our earthly goods inside a U-Haul truck, loaded our two Keeshond dogs into the backseat of our Buick Skylark, and set off on a 750-mile journey from Arizona to a new home in California. We left behind parents, brothers and sisters, and a host of friends, many we'd known since childhood.

Since then, our jobs, church commitments, children's school schedules, and, oftentimes, limited finances have kept us from venturing more than once annually across the Mojave Desert to visit loved ones. So we've relied mostly on letters and occasional phone calls to send and receive news about our families.

More than once, after a frustrating day of mothering three children, I've opened the mailbox and found an encouraging

note from Mom with a new recipe tucked inside and instructions to "try this out at the next church potluck." An unexpected card decorated with a cheery Bible verse from an old-time girlfriend has lifted my spirits during one of those days when everything has gone wrong. And a word from my mother-in-law that she will be praying for good results on an upcoming medical test has brought a peace to my heart.

These notes of love from far-off family and friends have served as a source of refreshment to me. Without them, I easily could have felt alone and discouraged, alienated and distraught over the miles that separate us.

Yet my greatest source of comfort and inspiration has been the good news from a distant place called heaven. Because I have chosen to believe in and live by the wisdom of God's Holy Word, the Bible, my heavenly Father has sent, sealed, and delivered to me His Holy Spirit who promises to forever be my Helper, my Comforter, my Encourager, my Strengthener.

With or without letters from my dear ones, I know that my Redeemer not only will refresh me each day, but He will restore my soul.

Thank You, Father God, for sending
Your Holy Spirit who indwells me always
and renews me each day.
Amen.

SOMEBODY NEEDS ME

Evelyn Christenson

Teach a child to choose the right path,
and when he is older he will remain upon it.
Proverbs 22:6, TLB

Inherent in each human being is the need to be needed. It gives us a sense of self-worth, a zest for life, and a reason for living.

In our prayer seminars we discover the worth of ourselves as we practice intercessory prayer. As the urgent and often heartbreaking prayer requests are handed in, pray-ers find—many for the first time—that someone really does need them, and their prayers.

Corrie ten Boom told me that when she was five years old and had just received Christ as her Savior, her mother said to her, "Corrie, now you are an intercessor." And she found that the people living around her home needed her prayers. What a great way for a little child to find her self-worth.

Trying to motivate and instill a sense of self-worth in teen-agers at a prayer seminar proved to be a difficult experience.

These were two hundred members of a confirmation class who, along with a church full of adults, were learning to pray. But their presence was not voluntary, and the paper wads, bubble gum, and paper airplanes displayed on the first night showed me what they thought of themselves as pray-ers.

At the second session one of them came to me with a prayer request. "My ten-year-old sister cannot hear," she said. Fearing I'd never be able to motivate them if God chose to answer some way other than healing her sister. I challenged those two hundred teenagers by giving them the request. I told them it was their responsibility to do whatever they chose with it. I held my breath all that next week waiting for the outcome.

At the next session I found myself surrounded by a whole gang of the girls' teenage friends as she excitedly announced, "Guess what happened to my sister? She can now hear without her hearing aid!" Those two hundred teenagers had found the worth of themselves to someone in need.

After the last session of that prayer seminar, the pastor's wife came to me with tears in her eyes. "Do you remember the boy who was shooting paper airplanes and paper wads that first night? (How could I forget him?) Do you know what he just prayed in our little group? He prayed, 'Dear God, please teach my dad what You've just taught me!'

Thank You, Lord, for the way You answer
prayer. May this experience remind me of
the wonderful adventure of becoming
intercessors for others.
Amen.

KIND
WORDS,
HAPPY TEARS

Kay David

Heaviness in the heart of man maketh it stoop:
but a good word maketh it glad.
Proverbs 12:25, KJV

Can the words of a little child change a heavy heart into a glad heart?

Recently, after a hurtful situation, I left for church. Driving down the highway, I cried, "God, I can't teach today."

Arriving at church, I wiped my tears, prayed for help, and headed to the classroom to sow seeds of Jesus' love to fifteen two-year-olds. Little did I know the impact Matt's words would play in healing my heavy heart that day.

Matt had been attending my class for six months. Greeting him at the door with "Hi, Matt" and saying "Bye, Matt" as he left, brought no response. Although he participated in the activities, to my recollection, he never spoke to anyone in class.

"Story time," I called to the children. We gathered in a circle. "Sit up in your chairs like tall trees, feet still, and hands in your lap. Look at Teacher Kay, turn on your ears, and let's zip the lip. Story time is Teacher Kay's time to talk and your time to listen." Or was it?

With several eyes focused on me, and some lips zipped, I began. "Jesus is a special friend. He . . . " Halfway through, Matt, who was sitting next to me, looked up into my face and said, "Teacher Kay, I wheely love you." I was stunned. Matt's first words in class were some of the kindest a human can say. Five words describe my reaction: tears, tears, and more tears.

After gaining some composure, I said, "Boy and girls, Matt's kind words made happy tears come out of my eyes. Can you wait a minute till they stop?" Now fifteen pairs of eyes were fixed on me. You could have heard an ant walk across the floor. The children waited.

Matt's words brought healing to my heart. Isn't it just like Jesus to take something small and do a great big job with it? In the Scriptures, He took a little boy's lunch and fed a multitude, and with a two-year-old, the words "I wheely love you" turned a teacher's heavy heart into a glad heart. Aren't little ones precious?

Thank You, Lord, for the children.
Help me to be like Matt, free to tell those
I meet today, "I really love you."
Amen.

COFFEE AND
DONUTS

Josephine Davidson

So I came out to meet you, to look for you,
and I have found you!
Proverbs 7:15, NAB

It was September and the first day of school; for my children, the first day in a new school. We had recently moved from New York City to a suburb of San Francisco. All the necessary health forms had been signed, and the school transcripts were in sealed envelopes. We were ready.

I parked the car in the school parking lot and lifted my wheelchair out of the front seat, and then lifted myself into it. Mary Helene, Jim, and I went into the office where we were greeted by the principal and the school secretary.

Leaving the children in good hands, I got back into the car. As I drove out of the parking lot, I realized that my car was the only car leaving. Looking around, I noticed other mothers walking together. My eyes followed them to the auditorium where they climbed three steps before disappearing through

the doors. Three steps! I drove home, tears streaming down my face.

Shortly thereafter, as I sat sobbing in the kitchen, the door-bell rang. A woman I had seen in the school parking lot stood on the threshold with a bag of donuts in her hand.

"You couldn't come to the donuts, so the donuts came to you."

"Thank you," I said as my voice caught.

"Come on," she suggested, "let's make some coffee."

This wonderful woman, Verna, had seen me go into the office in my wheelchair. She had recognized my car, with out-of-state license plates, as having been parked in a driveway near her home. Without a thought about herself, she skipped the yearly ritual of coffee on the first day of school, stopped at the donut shop, and came to visit me. I love her for it.

Our friendship was sealed that day over coffee and donuts.

Thank You, Lord, for showing me what
empathy means, that reaching out to
others is reaching out to You.
Amen.

THE WISEST
COMPANION

Beverly Eliason

He who walks with the wise grows wise,
but a companion of fools suffers harm.
Proverbs 13:20

Sharon twisted her legs into a pretzel knot. She stared at the floor, avoiding my eyes. Only three months after her release, here she was, back inside.

As I passed out hymnbooks and Bibles, I asked myself, "Why did I ever get involved with prison ministry? These girls break my heart."

Sharon had seemed sincerely repentant. She came from a good background and had the support of Christian parents. If she couldn't make it, what hope was there for the others?

The last of the inmates straggled in to the little, white-washed chapel. A guard shut the door behind them.

They formed a small island of women in a prison designed for men only. Most of them were young and scared. Some reminded me of my own daughters.

We opened with a circle of prayer. Sullen faces softened. Flute-like voices rose in well-loved hymns.

My eyes were drawn toward Sharon. *She must have fallen back in with her old crowd*, I thought. It happened over and over. Good intentions couldn't stand up to bad companions.

Sharon lifted her red-rimmed eyes. As she praised the Lord in song, her face seemed lit with an inner glow. I caught my breath. Could this be a real breakthrough? Or was it just another false start?

"Dear Lord," I whispered, "what can I do to get through to her?" I felt so helpless. "Does anything I do here really matter?"

The women sang on. I felt God's peace take hold. "What are you telling me, Lord? I think I see. I can offer Sharon friendship. I can steer her toward Christian companions. Maybe I can lead her one step forward in her walk with You. The rest I have to leave in Your hands."

I smiled to myself. I was turning her over to the wisest Companion of them all.

The women joined hands for the final prayer. I hugged each one as they filed out. Sharon gave me her sweet, childish smile. I held her for a moment, then surrendered her to His care.

Dear Lord, help me never to forget that any
good that I do in Your name comes only from
You and not from my own strength.
Amen.

THE
AIRPLANE
TICKET

Pamela Farrel

The mind of man plans his way,
but the LORD directs his steps.
Proverbs 16:9, NASB

I checked my ticket one last time before boarding with my two small sons. Arrive 10:50; Depart 1:10. I whispered a prayer, "Lord, walk us through. Get us there safely."

The first leg of our trip was relatively uneventful. I did enjoy conversing with an elderly woman in the seat beside me. She noticed I had my hands full with my two children and invited us to use the sky cab that was to help her to her next connection. Knowing we had hours to kill, I accepted.

We left the plane last and waited only minutes for the sky cab. I told the driver to please get my new acquaintance settled first. We all zipped down the hallways and deposited her safely at her gate. He then asked me for my ticket. I handed it to him, rattling on about how it would be nice to know if there was a quiet place to nurse my baby. He looked at me in disbe-

lief, "Lady, you'll have to nurse that baby on the plane! Your plane is leaving NOW! HOLD ON!"

He whizzed down the corridor while he radioed ahead to hold the plane. I gazed at my ticket. Arrive 10:50; Depart 11:10. I'd looked at that ticket at least ten times in the last twenty-four hours, each time reading it wrong. All I could manage to get out in those few seconds was an "Oh, Jesus, help us!"

The plane reopened its doors to let me and my tousled children aboard. I plopped down in my seat and deposited my toddler next to me. I began to weep. The people around me began to ask, "Are you okay?" "Can I help?" "What's wrong?"

I blurted out, almost shouting with joy, "My God is so good. Let me tell you what great thing Jesus just did to get us here!" I recounted the story, with half the plane listening by this time. I didn't care if they thought I was emotional, or that I was a dizzy blond who couldn't read her ticket. I had a personal God who cared enough about me to answer what I muttered as a sincere but seemingly insignificant prayer. I had carefully plotted and rehearsed the steps of my day, but God had gone ahead of me.

Jesus, help me never take for granted the
power and purpose of Your directing my way.
Take me through today Your way,
step by step.
Amen.

'Til Death Do Us Part

Carol L. Fitzpatrick

May your fountain be blessed,
and may you rejoice in the wife of your youth.
Proverbs 5:18

When we said our vows twenty-five years ago, I had no idea what I was promising. I knew that I was "in love," and that that was supposed to be enough to cover any problems that surfaced. It wasn't enough.

Both of us had grown up in dysfunctional homes, and were sorely lacking in the equipping necessary to make our house a home. During the first year, we lost a baby, moved three times, made it through Army boot camp and then Officer Candidate School.

All the while, our emotions were out of control. He was always angry, and I was always sorry. However, the worst problem was that we suffered a deep spiritual void. We fought on the way to church and then again after the service.

Having three more children within the next four years, including one who was hyperactive, sent me over the edge. Then I broke my back in a sledding accident. During my long recovery, a loving neighbor reached out to help us physically. More importantly, she introduced me to the Bible. As I studied the Word, I found a compassionate Christ who not only saved me but wanted to help me live my life.

It took thirteen more years for my husband to find peace in his own Christian commitment. During that time I was nurtured by loving friends and through Bible study and Christian service.

As we renewed our wedding vows for our silver anniversary, I thought of the miracle God had performed in two stubborn people. He not only kept us together but has given us faithful hearts toward each other. My husband is still rejoicing "in the wife of his youth."

Lord, when things don't seem to go right in my marriage, please help me to stay one more day and to trust You with all my heart.
Amen.

A CHILD SHALL LEAD

Marilou Flinkman

Even a child is known by his actions,
by whether his conduct is pure and right.
Proverbs 20:11

As I peeled potatoes for supper, I thought about my friend Lori. Her house had burned down and they had lost everything. Silently I thanked God for my own house and for the things that made it a home.

"Mommy, where is David staying?" John's six-year-old voice broke into my thoughts.

"At the Connors' house." David and John had been friends forever. It was David's house that had burned down.

"Can we go see his old house?"

"I guess we could, but there isn't much left of it except a burned shell." I sensed the concern in my small son's voice and gave him a hug. "David is all right. No one was in the house when it caught fire."

"But where will he live now?"

"His mom and dad will find another house. Right now they are staying at Rachel Connor's." I smoothed John's hair back off his face.

"Can I go see him? I want to take him a present."

Puzzled, I asked, "What present? It isn't his birthday."

John bent down to pick up the truck at his feet. He had wanted that truck for months. Our budget was slim, but we'd finally managed to buy it for his birthday last week. "I want to give David my new truck."

"John, are you sure?" I was shocked. "You could give David some of your old toys."

"No, I want him to have my truck."

"But, John, that's your favorite toy."

He looked up at me with solemn eyes. "Didn't you tell me David's house all burned up?"

"Yes, this morning it was totally destroyed."

"Then David doesn't have any toys, and I want to give him my truck."

Tears filled my eyes. My son was ready to give his most precious possession to his best friend. All I had done was thank God it wasn't my house that burned.

I put the potatoes in cold water and dried my hands. "We'll have supper a little late tonight. Get your coat, and we'll go see David right now."

> *Lord, help me see and serve the needs of*
> *others. May my actions be pure and right,*
> *selflessly giving as Jesus gave.*
> *Amen.*

THE GARAGE-SALE COUCH

Jane Esther Fries

Do not withhold good . . .
when it is in your power to do it.
Proverbs 3:27, NASB

Kathryn looked gaunt as she approached me after church. Her normally glistening auburn hair hung listlessly.

"Hi, how are you?" I said.

"Not well at all," she said quietly, her voice quavering slightly.

"What's wrong?" I asked, shifting uncomfortably.

"My new job hasn't worked out. I have to be out of my apartment by Friday, and I have no place to stay." She looked at me with a glimmer of hope.

"Oh, that's too bad. I'm really sorry," I said, just as another friend interrupted our conversation.

All evening Kathryn remained on my mind. I sensed the Holy Spirit nudging me. "I have presented you with a need, and you have the means to help." It was true. I did live alone,

and Kathryn could sleep on my garage-sale couch until she found an alternative.

It seemed odd, though, that I would be the one to help. Kathryn and I had never hit it off, and had even competed for the attention of the same young man.

Still, I felt compelled to act. So I invited her over. "Here's where you'll sleep," I said, motioning to the turquoise couch.

Kathryn gratefully sank into one of the snagged cushions. It absorbed many tears her first sleepless night. I didn't know what to say to help her, so I simply listened as she talked for hours. As the days passed, I maintained my daily routine as much as possible. Kathryn observed me cook healthy meals, spend time reading God's Word, and keep my home and personal appearance neat.

I never directly confronted issues in her life. Yet daily she gained emotional and spiritual strength. Soon the couch cushions dried and the TV rested from its all-night vigils.

One evening I noticed she had purchased notecards for Scripture memorization. In addition, she had neatly organized her belongings, and her hair donned a pretty bow. I could feel it; my couch would soon be empty.

I genuinely missed Kathryn when she left. Later she told me that those three weeks had been a turning point for her. I had shared the things she needed most: myself and my garage-sale couch.

Lord, thank You for Your promptings to help
others. May I respond with a willing spirit,
trusting You for the outcome.
Amen.

PRAYER, SOMETIMES A SWIFT KICK

Mary Francess Froese

Wicked men are overthrown and are no more,
but the house of the righteous stands firm.
Proverbs 12:7

I was at the beach one morning, just walking and talking with the Lord, troubled over a friend who was experiencing deep personal pain, due much to her own stubborn will.

I began to see the ocean as God—mighty beyond description, ever present and ever powerful. When a wave of power rushed in, it covered and washed the sand. The Holy Spirit allowed me to picture my friend as a glassy smooth patch of sand. The beach (she) was once covered with rocks (sin), but through the mighty hand of God washing over her, the rocks were dislodged and finally drifted out to sea—gone forever.

On the patch of sand that represented my friend, there were only a couple of small pebbles left to hinder the glassy smoothness. I watched the waves wash up over those pebbles, and as the water slipped back into the sea those little pebbles held

snugly to the wet sand. I saw one particular pebble as her pride and stubbornness. Moving closer to that little pebble, the Holy Spirit said, "Your foot is prayer; kick it." I gave it a good kick, but it didn't budge. "In the name of Jesus, be gone!" I grimaced as I again kicked the pebble. This time it moved a few inches. I was a little amused at its stubbornness, then I thought of my friend, and I smiled. When a wave hit it and washed out, the pebble tumbled a few more inches and then again embedded itself in the wet sand. When the water drew back into the sea, I went to where the pebble was and kicked it really hard. This time it skidded way out to the water line.

I thought for sure at the next wave it would wash out. No such luck. "Susie, why do you have to be so stubborn!" I kept my eye on that pebble, and when the next huge wave receded, there that pebble still was. By this time it was almost to the water's edge so I had to risk getting soaked, but I timed the wave just right and ran out and kicked the stubborn thing again in the name of Jesus, then quickly ran back to dry land. The next wave thundered to shore and quickly receded, but not before I saw that little pebble tumble end-over-end into the deep water, swallowed up forever in the mighty ocean.

Before leaving the area, I looked back at the wet patch of sand. It was as though that pebble had never been there.

Father, thank You that You are always there
to help us dislodge the thing that stands
between us and You. Your grasp is firm; You
will not let us fall, as the wickedness
is wrested from our hearts.
Amen.

A GIFT OF FRIENDSHIP

Joy Anne Held

Reckless words pierce like a sword,
but the tongue of the wise brings healing.
Proverbs 12:18

"If you had enough faith, you wouldn't need this operation," my friend Bob said flatly when I told him and his wife about my upcoming surgeries. He meant well, but his words struck a heavy blow to my heart.

That's easy for him to say, I told myself as I left, *he's not the one faced with paralysis.* Tears coursed down my cheeks. I had hoped for understanding and prayer from my friends. Instead I had been judged.

I stared at my nearly useless hands. I no longer had any grip strength, and the pain was often unbearable. Since physical therapy had only worsened my condition, surgery became my only option, and even that held no promises. In fact, the doctor had warned me, the operation itself might just speed up the paralysis.

"If it happens in surgery, it'll be quick and painless," the doctor said. "If you don't have surgery, you'll be paralyzed anyway, only it will be a very slow and painful process." I felt alone and frightened. Why did I have to face this?

Just before I left on a Medi-vac flight for the hospital in Ohio, my friend, Teri, hugged me. "I know you must be really afraid, Joy, but remember that God has you in the palm of His hand." She smiled, then quickly wrote something on a piece of paper. "I have a little gift for you. God gave me this verse a few years ago, and now I'm passing it on to you. It'll be my gift of friendship to you. Whenever you start to feel overwhelmed, read it again. Hang in there, and, remember, you're in our prayers."

Teri's gift proved timely. My heart was comforted time and time again as I read the verse from Jeremiah 29:11, "'For I know the plans I have for you,' declares the LORD, 'plans to prosper you and not to harm you, plans to give you hope and a future.'"

The surgeries were successful, and I have regained most of the use of my hands. During my hospital stays, I not only learned to trust God more, but also took advantage of the many opportunities I had to witness to other patients about Him. My friend's special gift of love and healing had made such a difference in my attitude.

Lord, seal my lips from reckless words.
Teach me to speak words of love and
encouragement to those around me.
Help me to be sensitive to their needs,
and let Your love flow through me.
Amen.

MY MOTHER'S HANDS

Carolyn Henderson

From the fruit of his lips a man is
filled with good things as surely as the
work of his hands rewards him.
Proverbs 12:14

"Your mother is being admitted to the hospital again because of her cancer," my father told me over the phone. I sensed an urgency in his words, so I didn't wait for my husband to come home. Instead, I called a baby-sitter for my three children and went immediately to the hospital.

When I arrived, the nurses were already helping Mother into bed. This ordinarily routine task so exhausted her that she soon fell into a coma-like sleep. I pulled a chair up to the bed and got as close to her as possible. I took her hand in mine and sat there for some time listening to her labored breathing.

As I reminisced, her hands were the first hands I remembered. They were hands that held me, fed me, rocked me, hands that guided, taught, and corrected me. Memories flooded my mind, and tears flowed down my cheeks.

I thought of how my mother had taught me to sew. I learned, with the help of her hands, to button my clothes, and to tie my saddle shoes, which always came undone until she showed me how to double knot the laces. She taught me how to measure flour and roll out cookie dough so that it wouldn't stick to my grandmother's rolling pin.

I remember as a child the coolness of her hands against my feverish forehead. I remember the hot, chicken noodle soup steaming in a cup, complemented with saltines and a story-book about a brave horse; my mother would turn the pages slowly so I could see every picture.

But now it was she who was ill. What could I do for her? What good were my hands? I felt helpless. Then, gently, out of the stillness of that hospital room, the words that Jesus had said on the cross drifted through my thoughts. At His death He had said, "Father, into thy hands I commend my spirit." So now I repeated that prayer for my mother who couldn't speak it for herself. I said, "Father, into Your hands I commend my mother's spirit. Lord, I ask You to take her hand." A peace filled that sterile room.

My mother died that evening. And when she did, I believe the Lord was already holding her hand.

Lord Jesus, thank You for Your caring
presence when I feel so helpless. Help me
remember that it is in Your love-scarred
hands that You hold mine.
Amen.

FREE TO GRIEVE

Joyce A. Hodson

Being happy-go-lucky around a person whose heart is heavy is as bad as stealing his jacket in cold weather, or rubbing salt in his wounds.

Proverbs 25:20, TLB

Shortly after our high school graduation, my boyfriend's eighteen-year-old sister committed suicide. Family and friends were devastated at the sudden loss of one so young and vibrant.

Many weeks after the funeral, Bob continued to mourn his sister's death. In my happy-go-lucky and positive attitude, I decided it was my job to help him snap out of his depression, to prevent long-term emotional damage.

Being a novice to death, I did not realize that grief is the human response to loss. I also did not recognize that it takes time to recover from the feelings of emptiness, sadness, and helplessness when we lose someone we love.

Although my intentions were good, I was "rubbing salt in his wounds" by not allowing Bob the freedom to grieve. A few

years later our relationship ended, with neither of us really understanding or accepting one another.

Since that first encounter with death, I have learned, through the loss of my own family members and close friends, more about coping with grief and emotions. I have learned, in order to start the process of healing, not to deny mourning, but to encourage myself and others to acknowledge our feelings, confront our losses, and express our pain.

Experience has taught me, too, that the best way to comfort a person with a heavy heart is to encourage him to look to Jesus Christ for hope—hope that admits pain is present, but that ensures it will not last forever.

Dear Lord, help me to be a comfort to
those who are grieving. Help me not to
judge their feelings, but to permit them
to be themselves. And thank You, Lord,
that through You I have hope.
Amen.

LIFE ROW

Janalee Hoffman

The teaching of the wise is a foundation of life,
turning a man from the snares of death.
Proverbs 13:14

As our prison ministry to death row entered its fifth year, we received a six-word note from a prisoner in Colorado, "Do you think God wants me?" I surmised that he was really saying, "I've done something so terrible that I'm not sure God will forgive me."

Those six words inspired a six-page letter back to him. As I prayed for wisdom, the Holy Spirit seemed to pour words through my pen. "Gary," I wrote, "if you saw a brand-new baby lying on the floor, cold, hungry, scratched, skinned up and dirty, would you make someone give that baby a bath before you'd pick it up? You wouldn't care about the dirt, would you? If that baby raised its arms to you, you'd pick it up, wouldn't you, Gary!"

And that's how God is with us. If we cry out to Him, He will pick us up, warm us, feed us, and fix all the places we're hurting.

I urged this young man to confess his sins and invite Jesus into his heart so that death row could be transformed into "life row."

Oh, what joy I felt as I read his return letter. "Jan," he wrote, "I kiss the chains I wear, because I now wear them for Jesus! I may be condemned by men, but I am loved by God. There is a quarter-size hole between my cell and the cell next door, and I have been reading my Bible to the prisoner living there. Frank accepted Jesus as Lord of his life today."

> *Lord, we are all on death row until we*
> *have stood at the foot of the cross. Thank*
> *You for giving a person as ordinary as I*
> *the wisdom to help lost souls find their*
> *way home to You.*
> *Amen.*

A TALE OF
TWO HOUSES
Starrlette L. Howard

He that handleth a matter wisely shall
find good: and whoso trusteth
in the LORD, *happy is he.*
Proverbs 16:20, KJV

For many years an elderly lady in our neighborhood was noted for her beautiful tulip garden. Just passing by the colorful display made the heart want to sing; her garden represented earth's beauty at its best.

Next door to her was the unkempt home of an old bachelor. His fence was battered and broken, weeds shot up everywhere, and the paint was peeling.

Such extremes of appearance, it seems, could not coexist for long. Neighbors wondered why the elderly lady didn't complain or make a phone call to the city officials. Yet no confrontation ever occurred. The beautiful tulip garden and the messy yard remained the same year after year.

But this spring an odd thing happened. As I drove down the street, I was surprised to see a few brilliantly colored rows of

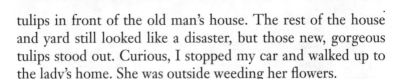

tulips in front of the old man's house. The rest of the house and yard still looked like a disaster, but those new, gorgeous tulips stood out. Curious, I stopped my car and walked up to the lady's home. She was outside weeding her flowers.

"Hello!" I greeted her. "I've always admired your beautiful tulips."

"Well, thank you," she said, smiling in a way that made those gray-blue eyes of hers twinkle. "If you'll wait a minute, I'll cut some for you to take home. They don't last long, mind you, but they sure brighten up a room!"

Within a few minutes she had cut a dozen gorgeous blooms for me. I thanked her and then said, "I noticed your neighbor planted tulips too."

"Oh, no," she said, winking at me. "I planted those for Mr. James. He lost his wife a few years ago, and his children have all grown and moved faraway. He lives such a bitter, lonely life," she sighed. "I call that a plot of hope."

"A plot of hope?" I asked, not sure what she meant.

"Yes, to give him back the hope that his own home can be beautiful again, that there is still goodness in life, and to let him know that God loves him just as much as He loves me."

I clutched my bouquet of tulips and left that garden feeling I had learned much more about the meaning of brotherly love.

> *Dear Lord, remind me that handling a matter*
> *wisely is to do so with kindness. Let me offer*
> *hope instead of criticism.*
> *Amen.*

SOUND
JUDGMENT

R. Ann Howell-Stump

An unfriendly man pursues selfish ends;
he defies all sound judgment.
Proverbs 18:1

Time was running out. I would barely make it to the meeting on time. I was exceeding the speed limit just slightly, while volleying my vision between the road and the rearview mirror.

Briefly, but unmistakably, she came into view—the lady with a flat tire. *Too bad!* I thought. *She must feel terribly frustrated. Oh, well, there will be others passing by. They can help her,* I rationalized.

I arrived at the agency where my office was headquartered, hurriedly found a parking place, then stepped from my car, gathering up papers with one motion.

It was then that the uneasy feeling in the pit of my stomach blossomed into a full-fledged anxiety attack, or was it budding guilt?

"Why not!" I heard myself say as I got back into the car and drove back to the flat tire scene.

To my surprise, the lady was still there, with the squalling toddler in the backseat, which my eyes had managed to miss the first time I drove by.

The lady looked as tired and haggard as I felt, maybe more so.

"There's a service station just up the way," I said. "I'll be glad to take you there."

In no time her toddler was transferred to the backseat of my car, and we were on our way. We began talking, "I hope I haven't inconvenienced you," she interjected.

"No problem," I responded, "I just need to make a call when we get to the service station."

After a few brief rings, the department secretary's voice came on the line. "Oh, you didn't get the message," she said. "The meeting has been canceled."

Dear Lord, help me to be less burdened down
by my own needs and self-interests, to look to
You for guidance, and to consider all the facts
in order to make sound judgments.
Amen.

WOULD YOU LIKE MY BANANA?

Bonnie Griffith Jamison

*Ability to give wise advice satisfies
like a good meal!*
Proverbs 18:20, TLB

Not long after we were airborne, lunch was served, but my eyes remained fixed on a book I was determined to finish reading. That was, until I heard, "Would you like my banana?"

Thanking the young man sitting next to me, I respectfully declined as he returned a heart-stopping smile. Exchanging names, Tom and I began chatting like old friends.

When I explained the subject of the book I was reading, it seemed to open the door for him to share with me about his troubled family background. Tom's childhood experiences had obviously left deep wounds that had not healed. I told him I understood. "You look like such a together lady," he said, surprised that I had knowledge of such trauma.

As the conversation continued, I broached the subject of Tom's spiritual life. He willingly said he'd once been a regular

church attendee, but admitted that presently his "religious life" was unfulfilled. "Having faith is important, but I know nothing about the Bible, God, or Jesus," he said.

When I explained that the Bible was a guidebook to life and that in it God speaks about His love for us and His plan for our lives, Tom's curiosity heightened. "The reason Jesus came to earth was to take away the sin that we're all born with. We simply need to accept Jesus personally. Then the consequences of sin are removed, and we're given freedom to live the way God wants us to." Hanging on to every word, I could see relief reflected on his face. I knew of an excellent church in his area and suggested that he try it.

By the end of the trip, I still hadn't completed my book. But, something far more important took preeminence that day. You see, because of a banana and a genuine smile, God gave me a precious opportunity to point this young man in the direction of heaven.

Dear Father, thank You for making me
sensitive to Tom's hunger for truth and
for giving me the wisdom to share
Your love so freely.
Amen.

GRAMMA, SING TO ME AGAIN

Sandie Jarvis-Dye

The righteous doth sing and rejoice.
Proverbs 29:6, KJV

My eyes grew heavy, and my body relaxed deeper into the warm covers as Gramma sang about Jesus and joy, and about someday going to heaven. Her soothing, gentle fingers ran across my forehead. Her soft voice slowly faded as peace engulfed me and I drifted into sleep. I didn't hear her say, "Goodnight, honey, I'll see you in the morning," as she tiptoed from the room.

But I did see her in the morning. My morning, however, came later than hers. By the time I got up, she had already showered and dressed, read her Bible and was fixing breakfast, humming a hymn.

Years later, I was the grandma with a tender lullaby and gentle fingers to caress a child's brow. I rocked slowly and sang softly about Jesus, till my tiny grandson drifted into a peaceful

sleep. After carefully laying him in his cradle, I kissed his soft cheek and tiptoed from the room, praying I, too, would follow Gramma's example and be a righteous influence on him.

Yesterday I sang to Gramma. Her eyes were closed, as if in sleep, as I stroked her forehead one last time. I leaned very close and my voice trembled, but I'm sure she heard me sing about heaven. My voice cracked and faded and tears filled my eyes. Though grief tore at my heart, I was happy because I knew that she was finally seeing heaven. For Gramma, the song was now reality.

I whispered, "Goodnight, Gramma, I'll see you in the morning," and quietly tiptoed from the room.

It will be awhile before that morning comes for me, but because my righteous Gramma taught me about Jesus, I know it will come. She's already there waiting for me. And I'm going to ask Gramma to sing to me again.

Lord, thank You for being Gramma's song
of joy. Because of her I now sing
of You to others.
Amen.

MY PLANS,
OR GOD'S?

Alyce Mitchem Jenkins

Commit to the LORD whatever you do,
and your plans will succeed.
Proverbs 16:3

I had important plans for the writers' conference. I'd meet editors, be inspired by speakers, and network with other writers. Before I went, I said my usual prayer: "Help me to do Your will. I'm Yours, Father, use me."

But I forgot God's role in my day. Instead, I became discouraged. Other freelancers monopolized the editors; successful speakers depressed me; and I met no helpful writers. Finally I retreated to Penn Station, feeling like I'd wasted both money and time.

The train to Newark was crowded. But on the local train, I faced an empty seat, until a young woman interrupted my reading, "May I sit here?" she asked.

"Of course," I nodded, absentmindedly.

As the conductor approached, I studied the young woman's face more closely. Her huge, brown eyes were filled with tears. "Everything's gone wrong today," she said, apologetically.

Dear God, what should I do? I prayed.

"Do you mind if I eat?" She pointed to a white paper bag on her lap.

"Of course not," I responded.

But she had difficulty swallowing the pizza.

"If you feel like talking, I'll listen," I said.

"Oh, it's too complicated," she replied. And then the words poured out, as she described problems no young person should have to face. Occasionally, I asked questions or offered encouragement. Mostly, I listened. Gradually her tears abated and her eyes brightened. "I know I can deal with things," she said as her station approached.

And then I took a chance. "I'll pray for you," I said. "I'm a Christian, and I pray every day."

"Thanks for listening. It helps to know that someone cares and is praying for me," she said, her eyes now shining.

"God bless you," I replied. And my heart went with her as she walked out of my life. But she didn't walk out of my memory. I've prayed many times for her safety and healing.

And what about my plans that day? Well, I didn't accomplish those. But perhaps on a day I had committed to God, His plans did succeed!

> *Dear Father, help me to look beyond my*
> *narrow goals and to commit myself to You,*
> *so that Your plans can succeed through me.*
> *Amen.*

THEIR DEATH WAS ONLY A BEGINNING

Barbara Johnson

The fear of the LORD leads to life;
and he who has it rests satisfied.
Proverbs 19:23, RSV

When our son, Tim, and his friend were killed, we learned that his VW had been smashed to bits by a three-ton truck driven by a drunken sixteen-year-old. In those first days after the accident, I felt such wrath that some drunk could cross the center line and send two boys into eternity. Yes, I knew that while their crushed bodies were left in that VW, their spirits had been ushered immediately into God's presence. Nevertheless, anger boiled within me. How unfair! How wrong!

A lot of my anger was directed toward God. For at least two weeks I drove to a nearby dump late at night to sob and sometimes scream out my rage. How could God do this again? Hadn't we had enough pain with my husband's accident and the death of my son Steve in Vietnam? But now this!

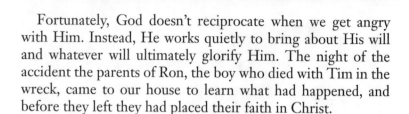

Fortunately, God doesn't reciprocate when we get angry with Him. Instead, He works quietly to bring about His will and whatever will ultimately glorify Him. The night of the accident the parents of Ron, the boy who died with Tim in the wreck, came to our house to learn what had happened, and before they left they had placed their faith in Christ.

A day or so later, Tim's picture appeared in the local paper with a headline that said, "Two Local Boys Killed on the Alaska Highway." In no time, several darling college girls began coming to our home to show me letters Tim had written to them the day before he started home. Tim's letters told the girls about his experiences that summer and how God had become real to him. These girls were eager to know more about the kind of God that could turn Tim on like that, and at least two of them accepted Christ right there in our home.

It was then that I began to see through my pain and grief and to realize that the death of my son and his friend might be an end to their lives here on earth, but it was just the beginning of their work here. The next week we held a memorial service that was attended by nearly a thousand people, and later we heard still more reports of how others who had attended the service had been touched by the Savior.

Though my grief was still very real, I began to understand that, in God's economy, the timing of my son's death was right. My anger dissolved as I saw others accepting Christ because of Tim's testimony.

> *Lord, thank You that I don't have to under-*
> *stand all that takes place in this lifetime;*
> *I just need to continue to trust You.*
> *Amen.*

A PROBLEM-
SOLVING GOD

Mercedes Johnson

The lot is cast into the lap,
but its every decision is from the LORD.
Proverbs 16:33, NKJV

I have a multichemical hypersensitivity and environmental illness, which keeps me fairly isolated in my home. My immune system has thrown up its hands in surrender because it can no longer function against the pollutants of this earth. I can't be around perfume and scented products or any chemicals. I can't go to shopping malls or talk on a plastic telephone.

In addition, my body cannot tolerate gas, natural or propane. I can't work outside my home, so when I had to convert my kitchen from gas appliances to electric, money was short. While I was pondering and praying about how this could be done, I received money specifically donated to help purchase a portable oxygen setup, as well as to make the kitchen conversion. But it was likely that the cost would be double the money I had received.

Now I needed the oxygen for when I left my home. And I needed an electric stove for cooking. Which one could I give up? I talked to the Lord about it and felt as if He were saying, "Don't worry." Although confused, I started making plans for both.

While searching one day in a store for a stove and feeling discouraged at the prices, I overheard a man ask the salesperson if they would buy his used electric stove. He was converting to gas because his wife didn't like electric. I ended up buying the man's stove, which had both the exact features and color I wanted. I also needed a stove hood, but the store was out of the one I wanted. So by taking the floor model, they took $100 off the price.

And, the electrician, a stranger to me but not to our Lord, refused to charge for his time when he learned about my illness; he said the Lord had never failed to bless him when he gave to others. I paid only for materials.

Yes, my lot had been cast into my lap, but God was there in the decision making. He met my every need by providing the money, and then by pointing me to the right place, at the right time, and to the right people.

Father, when problems tend to overwhelm me,
thank You for reminding me that You're a
problem-solving God.
Amen.

STAYING ONE-UP

Carole Turner Johnston

If your enemy is hungry, give him bread to eat;
and if he is thirsty, give him water to drink;
for you will heap coals of fire on his head,
and the LORD will reward you.
Proverbs 25:21–22, RSV

"Why didn't you call me? You knew you were going to be late! Why can't you ever think of anybody but yourself?"

I'd done it again. I just couldn't let the moment go by without trying to get even. I had gone almost three weeks on my new program that I called "doing the opposite." And now I had taken a step backwards. Well, I'd just have to record that, too, in my journal where I keep track of my successes, the times I've acted in accordance with Proverbs 25:21–22.

Since I can remember, I've needed to set the record straight, to maintain my own system of justice. But Proverbs shows a better way, one that's working for me, not only with my enemies, but with my friends too.

During the first week of my program, a close friend forgot our luncheon date. As usual, I began to feel the heat of retalia-

tion building up inside me. My ears started burning (that's how I know I'm getting ready to do something about an injustice). But this time was different. Instead of holding a grudge or refusing to set another date, I tried something new. I thought of the reference to bread in Proverbs 25:21 and baked brownies for her family, who seldom get homemade treats because of her busy schedule. Doing the opposite actually made me one-up, and it made everyone feel good, including me.

The next opportunity came two days later when a neighbor's dog got into my garbage again. Now, the old me might've taken my garbage and set it in front of my neighbor's house. But according to my program I was to give good for evil. I had it! The dog was probably hungry, or it wouldn't have gotten into my garbage in the first place. The next time I was at the store, I found a sack of dog food on sale, so I bought it and took it to my neighbor, asking her to try it out on her dog. Garbage days haven't been perfect since then, but I feel good about what I did and was one-up again.

The victories—or "coals of fire"— are growing and "glowing" in my journal. Now instead of reacting like I did in the old days, I read through my successes and gain new strength. And the Lord is already starting to reward me. I'm feeling much more peaceful, and my ears aren't burning nearly so often anymore.

Help me, Lord, to focus on the good I can do rather than on trying to get even. Help me to stay one-up in dealing with those around me.
Amen.

HEAVEN'S PHONE CALL

Joan Keller

Anxiety in the heart of a man weighs it down,
but a good word makes it glad.
Proverbs 12:25, NASB

Stressed and on the verge of burnout. That's exactly what I was feeling a few months ago as I mulled over the draining problems in my life. Working in the world's system and being a Christian is a continuous battle.

My appliances were on the blink again, and there was that unexpected car bill. To make matters worse, I'd come down with some strange inner ear problem that made me very ill for several months. In addition, my husband was ill. "Is anything going to go right?" I asked, as I wallowed in self-pity.

As my mind raced with anxiety, the phone rang. The last thing I felt like doing at the time was talking on the phone. Reluctantly I answered it.

It was long-distance, a woman from a Christian organization that I belonged to. At first I thought she was calling for a

donation. Much to my surprise she had called for one purpose, and that was to ask me if I needed prayer. Prayer! That's exactly what I needed.

She began sharing with me how good God is and what He had been doing in her life. She shared Scripture upon Scripture. As I drank in her words of encouragement, the tears streamed down my face. We must have talked for twenty minutes or more as she ministered God's sweet, calming peace to my heavy spirit. I could feel the burden being lifted from my being, and when she finished praying, the anxiety was gone—totally gone.

I was amazed at how God had sent a stranger from two thousand miles away, the exact moment I needed it, simply to meet my need. I rejoiced for weeks to think that God cared that much that He sent His angel of mercy. He did understand what I was going through.

> *Father God, I praise You for Your compassion*
> *and loving-kindness. Thank You for*
> *lifting my earthly cares and sending*
> *encouragement when I am in need.*
> *Amen.*

YES, MEG,
YOU ARE
SPECIAL

Carol Kent

To make an apt answer is a joy to a man,
and a word in season, how good it is!
Proverbs 15:23, RSV

Glancing at the clock and knowing time pressures were great, I discreetly scanned the room for the closest exit.

Within two feet of freedom, I felt a tug on my arm. Turning around, my eyes momentarily met those of my pursuer. She haltingly stammered, "I know you probably don't have much time, but could we talk for a moment before you leave? In your message today . . ." She hesitated again, trying to express her thoughts. I could feel myself pulling away, stepping slowly toward the door, avoiding serious eye contact, and casually glancing at my watch while simultaneously feigning interest in this woman's need.

She read my body language as easily as if it had been shouted through a megaphone. Backing off, she mumbled, "Oh, never mind. I know you're busy. It was nothing anyway. Thank you for coming today."

Caught! Guilty! Convicted! The words were reverberating like a hammer in my conscience, reminding me that my subtle pulling away from this woman had negated everything I had said in my presentation about how significant we are to God and how, in turn, we should practice the example of Jesus.

I had carefully reminded the listeners of the necessity to look closely at the life of Christ recorded in the Gospels and notice the way He responded to people. When He looked at individuals, He had kind eyes and empathy. He had a way of looking people in the eye and nonverbally communicating that they were important, valued, and significant.

Stabbed with a pang of guilt, I went after the woman and found a quiet place to talk. I was initially surprised by her lack of focused eye contact. For someone who had desired this meeting so much, she appeared unable to look at me for longer than an instant; then her gaze would go to the floor, to her lap, or to the wall. Without words, her behavior made a strong statement. She had no self-worth, and it had been a monumental act of courage for her to approach me.

She spoke with measured caution. "I'm Meg. I'm nobody special, and I shouldn't be taking your time; but I had to talk to somebody. . . ."

Dear Lord, give me the right words to speak
Your love to the Megs of this world. Thank
You for those opportunities to minister
to them in Your name.
Amen.

A PAUPER
TEACHES A
PRINCESS

Penny Kwiat

A generous man will prosper;
he who refreshes others will himself be refreshed.
Proverbs 11:25

Not long after we moved to the Northwest and settled in the parsonage beside the church, I noticed a young woman who came by everyday with her little boy, sometimes for lunch, sometimes to play on the playground. Their clothes old and their hair unkempt, they sat outside on the steps far from everyone else.

I was drawn curiously to the woman and her son. I'd smile and wave and, sheepishly, she would manage a smile. Before long she started coming to church. Some of the women were annoyed by her harsh tones and her unkempt ways.

One day, I invited Lisa to our women's monthly outreach meeting. She loved it and began attending month after month. During the sharing time Lisa would sometimes talk for thirty to forty minutes, though not a word was under-

standable. Some of the women walked out, some complained bitterly and left the ministry, while another group patiently endured my decision to continue to allow her to speak.

Week after week God gave me patience and endurance with Lisa. Little by little her speech improved, her nervous habits lessened, and she developed a love for the Lord.

In one of our intimate talks after her husband left her, Lisa shared, "I would watch you leave your house to go to the church. You looked like a princess coming out of a castle. To think the princess would take time for me means so much." Words cannot describe how that made me feel.

Two years later Lisa left our valley and went to live with her parents. She still phones, only now the conversation is different. "My son's doing well in school. I love college. And my new church and Bible study is wonderful. You know, because you were there for me I had hope when there was darkness all around me. Because of you I know there's a better way. Thank you."

Truly, "He who refreshes others will himself be refreshed!"

Lord, help me to love the unlovely. Help me to risk getting my hands dirty and losing pious friends. And help me to remember to thank You, Lord, for the blessings Your special people bring to my life.
Amen.

PORCUPINES

Cecilia Mainord

A wise man's heart guides his mouth,
and his lips promote instruction.
Proverbs 16:23

The simplicity of my son's discovery was so childlike, yet truth penetrated my heart in a challenging way. With great enthusiasm and bewilderment, he urged me to come outside to see the porcupine. Upon entering the backyard and gazing into the toy box, I found the creature that had been so innocently mislabeled. A caterpillar lay nestled against the side of the wooden structure, motionless and silent. Some things aren't always as they appear.

And so it is with people and circumstances. I have frequent interaction with large groups of people and am usually comfortable exchanging conversation with just about anyone, except one time in particular. A friend of mine was involved in a ministry at a prison camp for teenaged girls. Their offenses

ranged from selling drugs to prostitution to theft to man-slaughter.

I attended a Christmas program at the prison and felt comfortable until an invitation was given for all the guests to join the inmates for refreshments. Suddenly the reality hit. I would have to interact with girls with whom I had nothing in common. What would I say?

My heart was pounding, and my mind was racing. What were these girls thinking of me? Were they laughing? Or scoffing? Or criticizing? My naiveté immobilized me, and I failed to appropriate Scripture. If I would have asked for wisdom, the Lord would have given generously to me.

In my insecurity, I failed to see that I was surrounded by caterpillars. Through the eyes of my two-year-old, the caterpillar appeared sharp and poky. Through my eyes, these teen-aged girls proposed the same threat.

But I realized that inwardly, somewhere in their hearts, there is a tender place just waiting for someone to fill with love. Perhaps they could inflict pain, but the truth is that Christ's love can penetrate deeper than any of our wounds.

Lord, when my perception causes insecurity,
may my heart be wise to see every person
through Your loving eyes.
Amen.

THE
CHRISTMAS
GIFT

Veronica McNamee

Do not withhold good from those who deserve it,
when it is in your power to act.
Proverbs 3:27

Outside our window, feathery snowflakes floated softly down, covering crusted mounds of snow on the frozen lake. Inside, the excitement of Christmas Eve filled the air. Dinner was over, stacks of dishes finally washed, and gifts of all shapes and sizes beckoned from beneath the sweet-smelling tree.

Gift opening time! We trooped into the living room and chose our favorite viewing spot for the fun to come. The oldest of our five children was twenty-three and the youngest fifteen. They weren't exactly toddlers, but still very much into the spirit of surprise on Christmas.

As we settled in, our older son Brendan asked if he could give his gifts first.

"As you know," he said, "money is a little tight for me right now, but I think you'll enjoy this more than anything I could buy."

He put a lovely Christmas record on the stereo and turned out all but the Christmas tree lights.

"You'll have to sit on the floor in a circle. Then each of us will start with the person to our left and tell something we appreciate about that person, then the next person, and the next, until we've all said something about each member of the family."

An uncomfortable silence followed. We were always a noisy group around the dinner table, but this was different. Finally, Mom was selected to start. Time flew. Tears flowed. One after another, secret thoughts of thanks bubbled to the surface and spilled out in great cascades of love.

"You let me take the run-a-bout on the lake by myself when I was just a little kid. I'm not sure I would be that unselfish."

"You really care about me."

"You said no and stuck to it, though it would have been much easier to let me go."

"I know I can always count on you."

"When you say something, I know you mean it."

"I remember the time when you . . . "

Two hours later, seven happy, tear-stained faces beamed at one another. It had become so easy to say, "Thank you. I really appreciate who you are." What a wonderful gift—a perfect way to start our Christmas gift exchange.

> *Thank You, Lord, for teaching our family how*
> *blessed it is to give from the heart, for these*
> *are the greatest gifts of all.*
> *Amen.*

BLESSED
WAITING

Barbra Minar

My son, if your heart is wise, my own heart also
will be glad; and my inmost being will rejoice,
when your lips speak what is right.
Proverbs 23:15–16, NASB

I am about to become a grandmother. My first-born son is expecting his first-born son. And I have come to be a part of the last days of waiting to experience God's profound mystery of new life. How I want this child to be a blessed child!

Steven lays his wide, strong hand on his wife Kathy's stretched middle. Kathy invites me to touch. So, my palm next to Steven's, I spread my long fingers. I feel the rolling and kicking of the baby. The three of us laugh. I put my mouth close and speak softly to him. "Baby boy, this is Grandmother. Time to be born!"

As night gathers her skirts around us, I wonder if the birth will come in the dark hours. Prayers sweep over me like a wind. Prayers for Kathy and Steve. Prayers for my grandson. As I half sleep, memories of my children's births wash through

my dreams. I wake and listen. The house is quiet. I pray and sleep again.

At 4:00 A.M., I wake for good. Wrapping myself in a large pink quilt, I sit cross-legged on my bed, like I did as a young girl, and watch for the dawn.

Dear little boy. What can a grandmother-to-be offer you while we wait? I have helped your dad move his office downstairs to make room for you. I have made you a white teddy bear and a blue and white-striped crib ruffle. I have prayed for you to know God. I have prayed for your health and for your safety. I have prayed for you to know love. I know! I'll ask for a special blessing. Yes! Child, I pray God will bless you with wisdom. And I pray I will have the wisdom to be a blessing to you as Grandmother.

As I pull the quilt up to my chin and blink against the strong early sun spilling through the window, Steven calls, "Mom!" Slipping on my clothes, I hurry downstairs. The waiting's almost over. I rejoice!

Father, thank You for drawing me close when
I must wait. Thank You that I can ask for
the blessings of Your holy love and
wisdom for those I love.
Amen.

INHERITANCE

Lois M. Mulnite

Apply thine heart unto instruction,
and thine ears to the words of knowledge.
Proverbs 23:12, KJV

Auntie had always been an inspiration to me. Since her death, I have realized how much she has given me.

Memories? Yes! When I was a child, she brought me coloring books and crayons and brightly illustrated books of fairy tales, not knowing she was setting me out on a lifetime journey of painting and writing.

She took me by the hand and walked with me on clear, cold, wintry nights; I can remember how vast the sky seemed and how bright the stars were as she pointed out their various formations.

In the summer, even as a grandmother, she rolled with me and my children down the sloping lawn beside her country home.

Inspiration? Yes! As a child, I would wander up to her attic workroom, where I'd inspect the household objects she was painting, and I'd read her short-story manuscripts that were neatly rolled and tied with satin ribbons.

When I was older, and talked with her about my writing classes and workshops, she was joyous and encouraging.

"Wonderful!" she exclaimed. "If there's something like that you want to do, you should go ahead and do it." Wise words from a wise lady who lived them to the end.

In her mid-eighties, she made an intensive study of dinosaurs. She read books, made her own patterns, cut the pieces of gaily printed fabrics, sewed, stuffed, labeled, and mounted them on large pieces of cardboard for display.

Only three days before her death, I received a letter from her, one which I will always treasure. Even with several physical disabilities, she did not speak of pain, nor of dying; even then she was making arrangements for me to bring her dinosaur collection to her so she could exhibit it in the convalescent home where she was a patient.

As I approach my senior years, I remember Auntie and thank God for the gift she was to Him and the inspiration she was—and continues to be—to me.

Heavenly Father, I thank You for the
people You send into my life who inspire
and encourage me. May my life, too, be a
gift to You and to those who need to hear
Your inspiration and encouragement.
Amen.

WORDS
OF CHEER

Joyce Anne Munn

An anxious heart weighs a man down,
but a kind word cheers him up.
Proverbs 12:25

Preparing a meal for nearly thirty people is not a simple task. Two ladies in our church did just that when I asked them to help with a prayer breakfast for a group of educators in our local school system.

The breakfast was scrumptious with egg casserole and all kinds of fruits and rolls. Everyone present commented about the food and many personally thanked both ladies. I thanked them, too, and later wrote both of them a brief note.

The following week at church, one of the ladies, with tears in her eyes, hugged me and said, "Your note made my day. You'll never know how much it meant."

Her reaction surprised me. Even though I truly appreciated what she had done, the note was rather routinely written.

Suddenly in my mind I was hearing another person speak those same words to me, when about a year earlier I had sent a note of support to a local town leader who had been receiving some unjust criticism. And then another voice quickly crowded into my mind with almost identical words. This had been in response to a note to a man whose wife was terminally ill.

Were there other voices hidden in my mind? Surely more people in my circle of friends and acquaintances needed an encouraging word from time to time.

How often have I looked for a way to serve God or sought for a special way to minister His love? Have I overlooked a very simple way of sharing His love?

It's easy to express appreciation or concern orally. But I've learned that taking a few moments to put those thoughts in writing can reaffirm to a hurting person how much I really care and can show my friends how much they're appreciated.

Dear Father, make me aware of those who
need a special word of encouragement or
appreciation. Create in me a desire to meet
those needs with written words, then nudge
me to get it done.
Amen.

CLOTHED IN STRENGTH

Geraldine Nicholas

She is clothed with strength and dignity.
Proverbs 31:25

Mother-in-law jokes have always irritated me. Not because I'm a mother-in-law, but because their negative connotation never applied to my own mother-in-law. She was an active, vibrant, fun-to-have-around lady who deeply loved her family. She entered into all family activities with zeal and enthusiasm.

I will never forget the shrills of laughter resulting from her attempts to play floor hockey with our six-year-old son. Grandma was the goalie armed with a junior hockey stick and positioned in front of the improvised net, where she would try to block the shots of a sponge ball aimed at her by her grandson.

Because of her ability to laugh and enjoy life so fully, we all found her Christian faith attractive. The children shared freely their concerns, because they had confidence in her

prayers on their behalf. We all knew her faith was deep and genuine.

What devastating news it was to discover she had leukemia. As we watched her physical vigor diminish, it became evident that even that cruel disease could not snatch away her spiritual strength.

Her sense of humor and smile, which never faded, inspired courage. Her love for her Lord flourished. Her prayer time increased. Her faith remained steadfast. Her submission to God's permissive will produced a peace that passes understanding. Throughout her life, and even in death, she was clothed with strength and dignity.

What a legacy of faith and influence she left her family. What a blessing are those who model strength and dignity because of their close association with God.

Lord, thank You for the influence of those who walk close to You. Help me to be a positive model of faith and strength because of my intimate relationship with You.

Amen.

A
PRIVATE
HAVEN

Linda Conarty Nylund

A friend loves at all times,
and a brother is born for adversity.
Proverbs 17:17, NASB

Peggy fetched me from the train station, a mass of tired muscles, aching emotions. She took me to her own private haven of rest, her home. After bustling me and all my parcels into her guest room, she smiled at me and said, "I have a special surprise for you, a candlelit bubble bath."

Thick towels, a gleaming tub, and a heavenly scented candle flickering in the mirror. Could this be just a bathroom? It looked like royal chambers to me. Then came the greatest gift of all, her parting words: "Don't rush. Relax. There is nowhere to go, no reason to hurry. I deliberately planned this retreat into bubbles just to bless you. Enjoy!"

So I was obedient. I quickly slipped out of my wrinkled, dusty clothes and into that soothing bubble bath.

Such bliss to linger and soak, with bubbles tickling my face. The steaming water caressed me like velvet. As I soaked, tiredness began to seep out of my bones. In that blessed, quiet hush, I felt the dull pain of life being eased. My precious friend, how could she have known that one bubble bath could minister so? Though I sank into that tub a weary commoner, soon I would emerge a queen!

It was then that I reflected on another Friend. He, too, had prepared something special, something that would speak and minister to His loved ones—a gift that only He could give. Abandoning His robe, He took a basin of water and tenderly went to each disciple, washing and drying their feet. Though He was the one descended from royalty, He humbled Himself to allow rough and ragged men to feel like kings for one special evening.

So has my friend done for me. Out of her selfless, giving heart she has allowed me to feel like royalty. I see again how very like our Friend she really is.

> *Lord, please make me more like You,*
> *that I, too, may provide a haven of*
> *friendship for those in need.*
> *Amen.*

ERRING ON THE SIDE OF GENEROSITY

Fawn Parish

He that hath pity upon the poor lendeth
unto the LORD; and that which he hath
given will he pay him again.
Proverbs 19:17, KJV

We were traveling across America on a very limited budget as we crossed into hot, steamy Louisiana. Spying a rest area just ahead, I welcomed the opportunity to splash some cool water on my face. It was so humid, I didn't stop with just my hands and face. I got my hair wet too. As I glanced up from the fountain, I saw my husband talking with a man, and some sort of transaction was taking place. Back in the car I asked, "Honey, who was that?"

"Oh, just somebody needing a helping hand," my husband replied. Knowing the fragile state of our resources and the strength of my husband's generosity, I pressed further. "What sort of help?" I queried, afraid of the answer.

"He said he was out of gas and that he still had a long way to go. And his baby needed milk."

"His baby needed milk?" I asked incredulously. "Why, that's the oldest scam in the world. People in foreign lands rent babies so they can use that line!"

"But what if it's true?" he asked. I had no answer. Then he uttered a line I'll never forget. "I'd rather help ten men, knowing that possibly nine of them were false, than miss the opportunity of helping someone genuinely in need."

I was quieted by his wisdom. I remembered a time in Korea where a dwarf who was quite deformed came up to us. He handed us a piece of paper which said that due to his size and deformity he was unable to make a living for his family. The note continued: "Could you possibly see your way clear to help me?"

I had asked, "Do you think he's telling the truth?"

"Telling the truth? For heaven's sake, just look at him!"

I did take another look, and realized my heart had become calloused to another's misfortune. I was more interested in uncovering a scam than in discovering a need.

When I come to God with a need, He never makes me prove how desperate I am. He never forces me to document all the ways I have tried to address the issue. He never fears that in giving to me He will somehow have less. I like my husband's attitude. If you have to err, err on the side of generosity.

Father, thank You that You never make me
prove how desperate I am. You always meet
my cries for help. Teach me how to respond
to others in need with wisdom and
compassion. Give me Your heart.
Amen.

EXCUSES, EXCUSES!

Margaret Parker

The sluggard says, "There is a lion outside!"
or, "I will be murdered in the streets!"
Proverbs 22:13

"I can't be her friend," I told myself. "She is so sick she can hardly walk, and she lives right next door. She would be calling me all the time, describing her aches and pains in endless detail, complaining about her children, asking me to run errands. With the demands family and work make on me, I just don't have time for her."

That was how I rationalized my failure to reach out to Susan. I knew she had struggled with illness for years. On sunny days when I walked my dog, I sometimes met her making her slow, painful way down the block with her tiny dachshund. Our brief conversations were limited to small talk, but I liked it that way.

One morning she confided in me, "The days are so long when my husband is at work." I could read the loneliness in

her eyes, and I sensed God wanting me to be her friend. But in my mind's eye I could see my neighbor like a stone around my neck, dragging me down, preventing me from getting other important things done. Somehow I just never got around to asking her over for coffee.

Then one night I hard a siren and saw the flashing lights of an ambulance next door. "Oh no, Lord!" I prayed. "Don't let Susan die. I never really listened to her."

What relief I felt weeks later when I caught a glimpse of her shuffling down the sidewalk, hunched over a cane, her little dog at her heels. Again God said to me, "Be a neighbor to Susan." Even though she looked weaker and needier than before, I knew I must obey this time.

None of the daunting scenarios I'd visualized actually happened. Susan did not ramble on about her illness or complain about her children. She never once asked me to run an errand. Our visits proved to be a welcome break in my days.

How foolish my excuses must have appeared to God. By imagining "lions in the streets," I'd justified staying in my snug, safe routines. But He knew that when I stepped outside of myself to help Susan, I would find not the lions I feared, but deeper peace and a richer life.

Father, You are so merciful and mighty,
and the lions in my imagination are so
flimsy. Teach me to trust You and step
out fearlessly when You call me into
new paths of service.
Amen.

NEIGHBORS

Louise H. Rock

*Do not testify against your
neighbor without cause.*
Proverbs 24:28

Doing dishes is not one of my favorite things. But I didn't mind so much when, as I worked at the kitchen sink, I could look out the window at the willow trees and the lake beyond.

Then one day our next-door neighbors asked us to sign a petition. They wanted to add a garage with a second-floor room to their house, which meant that instead of my beautiful lake view, I would look out at the wall of their garage.

Since putting on the addition would bring their house too close to our lot line, they needed permission from our neighborhood governing association. If we, as their neighbors most affected by the addition, would sign the petition, the board would probably grant the variance. If, however, we went to the board and testified that granting the petition would lower

the value of our house, their request would most likely be denied. The result rested on our decision.

We didn't want the neighbors to build their garage. On the other hand, we wanted to be good neighbors. And we wanted to do what we felt was right in the sight of the Lord. So we didn't go to the governing association and object. Instead we signed the petition, and as we had expected, the board granted the variance. Then the unexpected happened.

The neighbors had done their homework; they had researched the cost of a garage addition and had put it into their budget. But when they asked a builder for a firm bid, it came back at twice what they expected. It turned out that the garage itself was only the beginning. The driveway, the second-floor room, and other extras doubled the price.

Our neighbors wanted the whole project, but felt it was too much money to invest in a house as old as theirs. So they never built the addition.

After that our neighbors seemed to view us almost with affection. In fact, when we decided to move, they decided to move too. They said that living there without us wouldn't be the same.

When we refused to testify against our neighbor, the Lord used it to our advantage. The neighbors were happy, and we still had our beautiful view of the willows and the lake beyond.

Dear God, help me to be mindful of my
neighbor's needs and to have the
wisdom to know when to put my
desires above those of others.
Amen.

THE LORD
DIRECTS

Alene Adele Roy

*A man's mind plans his way,
but the LORD directs his steps.*
Proverbs 16:9, RSV

My reservist husband, Tom, was called overseas suddenly, leaving me at home with our seventeen-year-old son. It became a stressful time; we both missed Tom desperately. Often my son and I would go to bed early, feeling ill. Other evenings I wrote letters to my husband, while my son did homework. Soon we weren't spending much family time together.

With financial and medical worries, plus concern for Tom's safety, my son and I weren't always in the best of moods. During the dinner hour I sat glued to the TV news coverage of the war, eating from a tray, while my son ate alone in the kitchen. He couldn't stand to hear the prolonged reports, while I, unfortunately, needed to hear everything.

It seemed as if our lives would never be normal again. Several times I suggested that we play games or go out to dinner,

but my son always dismissed my suggestions. He was "too tired," or he had "too much homework," or he didn't "feel like celebrating." I explained that eating out wasn't celebrating, but rather it was an opportunity to spend some time together.

Then, one evening a movie came on TV, and I saw my son settle on the davenport with his favorite pillow and blanket. I knew he'd be staying up late, a rare occasion, so I was now free to write letters, read, or enjoy a hot bath. But as I turned to go into my room, something changed my mind. Instead, I did what I think the Lord was directing me to do. I settled in my husband's big rocker with my own blanket.

Soon my son noticed me. "You don't have to watch this," he said. I answered, "But I want to!" Soon I was like a teenager again, now sprawled on the floor, watching the movie intently. During a commercial, I asked if he wanted popcorn. He seemed delighted. By the end of the movie, we were laughing, talking, and feeling happier than we'd felt in months.

I realized that this was the quality time I'd been wanting with my son. That night, through God's direction, we went from lonely military dependents to a family again.

Thank You, Lord, for directing my steps
when I would choose to go in another
direction. Thank You for reviving my
relationship with my son at such
a lonely time in our lives.
Amen.

THE
SWEETNESS
OF SUGAR

Jessica Shaver

*When you help the poor you are lending
to the LORD—and he pays wonderful
interest on your loan!*
Proverbs 19:17, TLB

A homeless woman taught me the truth of Proverbs 19:17. She lived in the parking lot behind a small office complex. I first saw her from the back, a bulky figure robed in many layers of clothing. Hooding her head was a heavy blanket, which was belted at her waist.

When she turned toward me, I realized with a start that she was beautiful, despite two broken front teeth. Her smooth, black face, clear eyes, and wide smile radiated an inner joy that made no sense in her stark circumstances.

I introduced myself. She said I could call her "Sugar." The following week, I brought her fruit. She said, "Praise the Lord!" but wouldn't take it. "I have fruit," she said.

On my next visit, I brought muffins, but she had bread. Once I offered her an embroidered handkerchief. She urged

me to keep it. Her gentle refusal told me that was not the kind of relationship she wanted. Once I didn't stop to speak with her. I only waved as I pulled into a parking space and dashed to an appointment. I had my own problems.

The next week was different. After several personal rejections, I was feeling bruised and fragile. I wanted to be around someone who would not expect too much of me. To my disappointment there was only a mound of gray clothing in the corner beside the shopping cart where Sugar usually sat. As I turned away, I heard a voice, and the mound of clothing sat up.

"Are you looking for me?" called Sugar cheerfully.

I sat beside her on a bumper in the broiling sun. She said the Lord was good, and I looked at her perspiring face and shopping cart full of old newspapers, the soiled blanket she lived in and the shoes on her feet, their tops only tenuously connected to their soles, the bags of stale bread, and the boxes of rotting fruit collecting flies.

I looked at this woman who had nobody and whose every possession could have fit on one shelf of my linen closet. She said she had been praying for me all week. I felt humbled. I had thought I was the rich one, but Sugar had given me more than I had given her. She taught me dependence, simplicity, contentment, and gratitude.

> *Lord, may I learn to look at those things*
> *You have chosen—the foolish, the weak,*
> *the base, the despised—for lessons*
> *You want to teach me.*
> *Amen.*

FOREVER PRECIOUS

Marcella Beecher Shaw

Her children arise and call her blessed.
Give her the reward she has earned, and
let her works bring her praise at the city gate.
Proverbs 31:28, 31

Sky Harbor's Terminal 2 seemed unusually busy as I hurried toward the lobby where travelers meet their hosts. The wait was not long. I watched attentively as the sky cap wheeled a frail, elderly woman down the ramp from the gate. She looked so small, so pale, yet she beamed with love and joy at seeing me. Her appearance, except for her eyes, gave no indication of the energy and courage that had marked her youth.

This was the woman who had raised five busy, noisy children. Who had laid the stone for a two-story fireplace in the mountains of Idaho. Who had cooked and sewn for scores of family members and boarders. Who had mothered forty newborn foster babies before they were adopted. Who had weeded and cultivated her garden in the hot Idaho sun. Who got up before dawn every morning for years to sign on the

programming for her Christian radio station. Who crocheted an afghan for each of her children and twenty grandchildren. Who had seen death take two husbands. This was the woman who had mothered my dear husband. At one time so strong, now she was so fragile and tremulous.

The years had taken their toll on her appearance, but they could not diminish her spirit. At eighty years of age she had a new house built for herself. She rode with her grandson on the back of a jet ski at a family reunion. She traveled the width of the country to see her children.

Nor could the years diminish her impact on the lives of those she loved. As a young bride, I learned from her how to can fruits and vegetables, how to freeze sweet Idaho corn, how to stuff and roast a turkey. I learned how to give a newborn baby a soothing rubdown. And inwardly, I struggled to emulate her quiet, patient spirit.

Nor will the years erase her memory. On the walls of homes and in the depths of our hearts, her gifts of love and wisdom have secured a place for her. In the courts of our Lord she will flourish forever.

> *Lord, may I be a woman known for works*
> *of faith and love. May my heart be turned*
> *to You and attentive to others so that my*
> *works will minister the eternal fruit that is*
> *worthy of the praise of my children and*
> *acceptable in Your sight.*
> *Amen.*

FOUND, AT LAST

Phyllis Shelley

Listen, my son, and be wise,
and direct your heart in the way.
Proverbs 23:19, NASB

My two dogs danced and barked excitedly around my feet as I slowly opened the front door. They didn't know who was waiting on the other side, but I knew. The first week in September always brought a "well-meaning" neighbor to my doorstep. It was Bible study time again. For the past three years my excuse had been perfect, but this year she knew that excuse would not work. I no longer could hide behind my Girl Scout leader role; I had resigned.

While Winnie petted the dogs, my brain wildly searched for some excuse, any excuse. None came to mind. After her loving invitation to join her the next morning, I promised to be ready at 8:30. I made up my mind that I would go three weeks and drop out. At least that might satisfy her.

The love, support, and acceptance I received from the group overwhelmed me. Even though I didn't understand words such as *justification, sanctification,* and *salvation,* the discussion was fascinating. My introduction to Christianity came through a study of the life and letters of the apostle Paul.

I struggled to understand the weekly assignments. I decided to hang in there awhile longer. After all, I loved to learn.

I will quit at Christmastime, I thought. The Lord heard my plan, but by Christmas He worked His plan.

On a December morning at Bible study we sang "Amazing Grace." "I once was lost but now am found, was blind, but now I see." Although I had sung the words of this hymn before, these words touched me in a new way. Tears of joy flowed. I realized I was no longer lost; I knew I could never live without Jesus Christ as my Shepherd and Savior.

After returning home that morning, I knelt by my bed. I prayed and cried, especially thanking the Lord for my persevering friend Winnie.

Soon after Christmas, another neighbor came to my door.

"Well, it's about time!" She laughed, greeting me with a big hug. "Winnie just told me the good news: You've become a Christian. I've been praying for you for eighteen years!"

Thank You, Lord, for Your persevering
messengers and praying friends who
never gave up on me. Through them,
I found Your love and Your way.
Amen.

"I'M SORRY I
HAD TO
SPANK YOU"

Judy Slotemaker

The rod of correction imparts wisdom.
Discipline your son, and he will give you peace;
he will bring delight to your soul.
Proverbs 29:15, 17

The immediate family gathered around my mother's hospital bed as she lay dying. She drifted in and out of consciousness as we filled her final days with favorite hymns and Bible passages, and recollections of a lifetime of loving family memories.

My brother, sister, and I voiced our appreciation of her consistent Christian testimony as we recalled a particularly shameful act of misconduct from our childhood.

We had played outside while Mother visited with her sister. Someone had found cans of motor oil and a can opener. We were gaily sloshing the shimmery liquid all over the carport of a brand-new home when the homeowner caught us.

The man was intimidating. A foot taller and a hundred pounds heavier than Mother, he informed her of our escapade in unbelievable crude language.

Calmly, she faced this irate stranger and addressed him gently yet firmly.

"I assure you my children will be punished at home," she told him, "but first they will spend the afternoon cleaning up the mess."

The man snorted a response laced with curses.

Mother breathed deeply. "As angry as I am with my children, I am equally saddened at the way you use my Savior's name. I cannot condone your language any more than I can excuse my children's actions. It hurts me to hear such vile abuse of the One who gave His life for me."

The fellow beat a hasty retreat, and we children spent the afternoon scrubbing.

As we smiled at the memory of Mother quietly bearing witness to that angry stranger, she slipped the oxygen mask from her face, slowly looking up at each one of us.

"I'm sorry I had to spank you," she said tearfully, then replaced the mask.

We laughed joyously for the first time that day. Mother had broken the tension and replaced it with joy and one final maternal reminder of the great truths of the Scriptures she loved so deeply.

Lord, thank You for godly parents who loved
their children enough to discipline them,
and to teach them to love You.
Amen.

FRIENDLESS—
OR WAS I?

Michelle L. Steinbacher

*A man that hath friends must show himself
friendly: and there is a friend that
sticketh closer than a brother.*
Proverbs 18:24, KJV

Moving three times in three years had begun to take its toll. In each new location I made a few new friends, but no friendship lasted beyond the next move. The only friendship I considered to be a lasting one had suddenly and severely deteriorated.

At the moment, I was in an unfamiliar town where neighbors were few and uncongenial. I was sad, hurt, depressed, and terribly lonely.

I certainly considered the Lord my friend, but the reality of His continuous presence in my life was something I lacked. It was during this time of loneliness that the Lord taught me what it means to have a friend that sticks closer than a brother.

About three months after moving, I accepted an invitation to take my boys, ages four and five, to Vacation Bible School

(VBS). My children had been to VBS before, but they seemed to have an especially good time this summer, which I suspected was partly due to the closeness in their ages and having been placed in a classroom together. One evening their teacher shared with me her observations about my children. "You know, your boys are always together," she said. "They're inseparable. In fact, they stick together like glue."

She proceeded to tell me how at Bible story time that night my youngest son was left without a seat because the chairs beside his brother were taken. The teacher explained how she tried unsuccessfully to coax my son to sit elsewhere, but he refused with a simple reply, "I can't. I have to sit next to my brother."

On the way home that night, I smiled as I pictured the scene. A four-year-old tagging behind his older brother, doing exactly what he did, refusing to sit anywhere but next to him. Brothers, inseparable, like glue. Yet Proverbs 18:24 says we have a Friend that sticks closer than all of that.

What a comfort those words became at my time of loneliness. Though friends were few, and I'd been sadly let down by others, I knew that, in Jesus, I had a Friend who would never let me down, and no matter where I went, He would go with me.

Lord Jesus, thank You for being that
Friend that sticks to my side like glue,
and for showing me that no matter how
lonely I feel, I am never alone.
Amen.

FORGIVE OR
SEPARATE

Dorothy Stephenson

*He who covers and forgives an offense
seeks love, but he who repeats and harps on a
matter separates even close friends.*
Proverbs 17:9, NAB

My closest friend was the one who had offended me, and I was having trouble covering and forgiving the offense.

From the minute of my friend's betrayal, I started crying and calling on the Lord. I could say with David, "I drench my couch with weeping" (Ps. 6:6).

I told the Lord how unfair it was. My wounds were deep and painful. The tape of "She said, I said" played hundreds of times in my mind, especially at night. I wasn't sleeping, and all my bones and joints hurt from frayed nerves. In short, I was miserable.

At the end of three wretched weeks, exhaustion brought my grieving to an end. Harping on this matter had kept me from hearing my dearest Friend, Jesus. I knew I could make the same mistake with human friends. Continual harping had

closed my ears from hearing any loving counsel the Lord wanted to give me.

Finally, I said, "Lord, what do You want me to do?"

He said, "Forgive her."

"Lord!" I exclaimed, "You know she is the one who should ask my forgiveness."

He reminded me how great my debt of forgiveness was toward Him compared to the minuscule debt my friend owed me.

Did I want sleepless nights, resentment, bitterness? Or did I want to cover that offense with forgiveness? The choice was mine.

I reached for the telephone to call my friend and seek love. How could I not, when He who is all love, continuously forgives and loves me?

Father, please help me to always choose
forgiveness, to lay my pride at Your feet,
and to never harp on anything,
except the wonder of You.
Amen.

No New Dresses?

Betty C. Stevens

*She opens her arms to the poor
and extends her hands to the needy.*
Proverbs 31:20

My mother loved to sew, but nearing eighty years of age she was slowing down. Always the perfectionist, she recently declared she was through sewing. She still had an interest in family affairs though.

My daughter and her husband often took used clothing gathered from several churches to a county seat in a needy Appalachian region of Kentucky. Returning from one such trip, they told of how little girls there usually begin school wearing hand-me-down, large-sized dresses belted over in the middle, so the girls wouldn't trip.

Mother asked, "Do you mean some of those little girls don't even have a new dress when they start school?"

"Grandmother," my daughter replied, "little girls down there hardly ever have a new dress."

The next day Mother said to me, "Daughter, get me some yard goods, and not all alike either. And a pattern. I'm going to make a dress or two."

Mother was slower in her sewing now, but she kept at it. Soon she had two cute, size-six dresses ready to be mailed to the school principal her grandchildren knew.

A grateful letter came back to Mother, describing the joy of two little girls who had their first-ever new dresses. That letter was read over and over.

"Daughter," Mother finally said, "I think you had better get me some more yard goods. And get some kind of fancy edging too. I guess my eyes and hands are good enough to keep making dresses for those little girls down there. As long as God keeps me able, I'm going to keep on sewing."

Thank You, Lord, for blessings of sight
and skills and energy. Thank You for
inspiring Mother and others to
keep on reaching out to the
poor and needy.
Amen.

THINK FIRST, SPEAK LATER

Nancy Witmer

When words are many, sin is not absent,
but he who holds his tongue is wise.
Proverbs 10:19

"What a stupid thing to do!" I spit out the words without thinking. "How many times have I told you to be more careful with your wallet?"

"I'm sorry, Mom. I forgot it was in my pocket when I jumped into the pond." My teenaged son withered under my scathing accusation and hung his head.

"Well, you can get a new driver's license," I said, "but I'm afraid your money is lost forever."

"The guys and I are going to go back and look for the wallet after school tonight," Richard said, as he picked up his books. "Maybe we'll find it."

"Fat chance," I muttered. "It's probably buried in the gook at the bottom of the lake." I watched my son walk dejectedly

toward the bus stop. *You shouldn't have been so hard on him,* my conscience prodded. *He just made a mistake.*

When Richard came home from school that afternoon, I apologized for my outburst and asked him to forgive me. "I spoke before I thought," I confessed. "I'm sorry."

That experience was only one bead on a long necklace of times when my agile tongue got me into trouble. I have a chronic case of speaking before I think. But the Lord and I are working on the problem.

Last night my husband admitted that he should have followed my advice on a recent financial decision.

"You were right," he said, "buying that truck was a bad idea."

The words "I told you so" leaped to my lips, but the Lord nudged me, and I swallowed them. When my husband glanced my way to see whether I'd suffered a swift attack of lockjaw, I only smiled and said, "I'm sorry, dear. I hope everything works out all right."

Speaking in haste often destroys relationships and inflicts emotional wounds. Contrary to what the rhyme says, words can cause as much, or more, damage than sticks and stones. I believe the wise man Solomon would have agreed with another wise person who said, "Be sure to engage the brain before putting the mouth into gear."

> *Lord, help me choose carefully the*
> *words I speak today. Let them bring*
> *wholeness and healing and hope.*
> *Amen.*

MEET OUR CONTRIBUTORS

DeLaine Anderson is a homemaker and part-time executive secretary who enjoys writing, gardening, home decorating, cooking, and directing a children's choir at her church. She and her husband, Ray, have four grown daughters and two grandchildren and make their home in Excelsior, Minn.

Delores Elaine Bius is a freelance writer, speaker, and writing instructor. She has published over 1,650 articles during her twenty years of writing. Delores lists as her hobby listening to classical music. She has five grown sons and four grandchildren and lives in Chicago, Ill.

Myra Boone is a support services specialist and professor of education at Azusa Pacific College. She helped write and present curriculum titled "Christian Morals and Ethics: A Foundation for Society" that was taken to Russia and used to train over five thousand educators there. Myra resides in Duarte, Calif.

Catherine Brandt is a homemaker who has written eleven books for Augsburg Publishing. She has one son and one daughter and

eleven grandchildren. Catherine makes her home in Golden Valley, Minn.

Georgia E. Burkett is a retired college faculty secretary who has written over one hundred devotions, a history of her hometown of Royalton, and several articles. She enjoys gardening, historical research, and needlework. She has six children, seventeen grandchildren, and eleven great-grandchildren and lives in Middletown, Pa.

Mary C. Busha is a freelance writer, the compiler of several devotional books, an instructor of writers' classes, and a speaker for women's groups. She also enjoys reading, traveling, and gardening. Mary has three grown children and two grandsons. She and her husband, Bob, make their home in Santa Rosa, Calif.

Barbara Caponegro is a homemaker, teacher, and freelance writer who enjoys traveling, reading, research, crafts, and learning. She and her husband, Patrick, have two teenaged children and live in Medford, N.J.

Irene Carloni is an article writer, scriptwriter, editor, and producer. She has received awards for her work with cable TV. Part-time caregiver of her handicapped son and volunteer at her church video ministry, Irene enjoys photography, crafts, and Bible study. The Carlonis have three children and live in Manhattan Beach, Calif.

Julie Carobine is a homemaker and freelance writer who enjoys running and coleading with her husband, Dan, premarital sessions called Down the Aisle. Julie has written numerous articles for various publications. The Carobines have two young children and live in Ventura, Calif.

Amelia Chaffee is a journalist and staff writer and editor for the U.S. Center for World Missions in Pasadena. She enjoys international folk music and dance, sampling ethnic cuisine, taking long bubble baths, and reading English mysteries. Amelia and her husband have two grown children and one grandchild and live in Fillmore, Calif.

Susan Childress is a freelance writer, university student, representative for AISE (a foreign exchange student organization) and a former daily newspaper reporter. She enjoys reading, traveling,

gourmet cooking, genealogy research, and writing letters. She and her husband have three children and reside in Modesto, Calif.

Evelyn Christenson is the author of *What Happens When Women Pray; Gaining Through Losing; Lord, Change Me; Battling the Prince of Darkness* (Victor), and more. Board chairman for United Prayer Ministries, she speaks to thousands every year on the topic of prayer. She and her husband, Chris, have three children.

Kay David is a Bible study teacher, writer, and retreat speaker who has had several devotions published. She enjoys reading and walking. Kay and her husband have two children and two grandchildren and live in Greenacres, Wash.

Josephine Davidson is a retired school teacher and now an advocate for the disabled, speaking on a variety of topics relating to those with disabilities and in wheelchairs. Besides writing she enjoys collecting dolls. Josephine and her husband, Peter, have two grown children and five grandchildren and live in Bellingham, Wash.

Beverly Eliason is an insurance broker who has written articles for several publications. Active in prison ministry, she and her husband have five children and three grandchildren and make their home in Newtown Square, Pa.

Pamela Farrel is a freelance writer and speaker and a director of women's ministries. She is coauthor of *Pure Pleasure: Making Your Marriage a Great Affair* (InterVarsity) and author of numerous articles. She enjoys swimming, skating, and reading. Pamela and her husband, Bill, have three children and live in San Marcos, Calif.

Carol L. Fitzpatrick is the author of numerous articles, poems, and books. In addition she is codirector of Christian Writers' Fellowship of Orange County and a teacher for Precepts Bible Study. Carol enjoys sewing, doll making, calligraphy, and baking. She and her husband, Joe, have three grown children and live in Lake Forest, Calif.

Marilou Flinkman is a speaker and writer of over one hundred short stories and articles. She enjoys fishing, reading, and white water rafting. Marilou has six grown children and nine grandchildren and lives in Enumclaw, Wash.

Jane Esther Fries, formerly a teacher, park ranger, and youth camp dean, is now executive assistant to the director at Warm Beach Christian Camp and Conference Center. She has written numerous articles and enjoys singing, playing flute and guitar, horseback riding, and cross-country skiing. She lives in Stanwood, Wash.

Mary Francess Froese has written numerous devotions and articles and is the author of *Heroes of a Special Kind* (Evergreen). She is secretary to a San Diego County supervisor and enjoys antiques, Bible studies, and speaking to Christian women's groups. Mary and her husband, Allen, have two sons and reside in Vista, Calif.

Joy Anne Held is a homemaker and freelance writer and editor who enjoys floral arranging, making floral wreaths, reading, music, hiking, and gardening. She and her husband, Joe, have one son and make their home in Pownal, Vt.

Carolyn Henderson is a graphic designer, who is interning to be a marriage, family, and child counselor. Author of several devotions, she enjoys painting, quilting, and "watching her family grow spiritually and physically." Carolyn and her husband have three children and one grandchild and live in Newbury Park, Calif.

Joyce A. Hodson is a freelance writer and speaker whose articles have appeared in a variety of publications. She is volunteer coordinator for her city, working with the mayor, council, and chamber of commerce to promote volunteerism. Joyce and her husband, Evan, have three sons and live in Killeen, Tex.

Janalee Hoffman is a jeweler and prison chaplain who has written two articles and the book *No Flowers for Their Graves* (Joy Publishing). She enjoys scuba diving and competing in pistol shooting events. Janalee has four children and nine grandchildren and makes her home in Green Valley, Nev.

Starrlette L. Howard has had articles, short stories, and poetry published in over one hundred publications. She enjoys baby and nature photography, embroidery, flower gardening, and publishing a holiday homemaker newsletter. Starrlette and her husband have five grown children and seven grandchildren. They reside in South Ogden, Utah.

R. Ann Howell-Stump is a speech clinician, working with middle and high school students. In addition to writing, she enjoys reading and traveling. She and her husband, Harold, have one grown daughter and live in Sioux City, Iowa.

Bonnie Griffith Jamison is the author of *Take Me Home* (Tyndale) and several articles. She enjoys speaking at women's retreats and banquets, reading, walking, biking, video photography and interior decorating. She and her husband, Ted, have three grown children and five grandchildren and live in Medford, N.J.

Sandie Jarvis-Dye is a medical transcriber, word processor, and desktop publisher. She has written several devotions and articles and enjoys biking and flower gardening. She and her husband, Nathan, have four grown children and four grandsons and reside in Wenatchee, Wash.

Alyce Mitchem Jenkins is a retired teacher and the author of several essays, articles, and short stories, which have appeared in a variety of magazines and newspapers. She enjoys reading, watching women's basketball, letter writing, and traveling. Alyce and her husband, Reese, have two grown children and live in Warren, N.J.

Barbara Johnson is the founder of Spatula Ministries. Ministering to hurting people all over the world, her books include *Where Does a Mother Go to Resign?* (Bethany); *Stick a Geranium in Your Hat and Be Happy;* and *Pack Up Your Gloomies in a Great Big Box, Then Sit on the Lid and Laugh* (Word).

Mercedes Johnson is the author of several articles and poems for newsletters and Sunday School teachers. She enjoys researching biblical history, reading, and desktop publishing. Mercedes and her husband, Jawn, have one grown daughter and one grandson and live in Oxnard, Calif.

Carole Turner Johnston is a freelance writer, photo journalist, and GED teacher. Her books include *Little Book of Holidays* (Fairway), *Cat of Many Colors* (Tiger Moon), and *Early School Houses* (Quixote). She enjoys jogging, reading, and taking nature walks. She and her husband, Terry, have five children and reside in Onawa, Iowa.

Joan Keller is an accounts receivable and marketing specialist for a physical therapy center and the author of poetry, articles, and devotions. She enjoys hiking, gardening, and basket making. Joan and her husband have one daughter and make their home in Boyertown, Pa.

Carol Kent is a freelance writer and speaker, and the founder and director of *Speak Up with Confidence* seminars. Her books include *Speak Up with Confidence* (Thomas Nelson) and *Secret Longings of the Heart* (Navpress). She and her husband, Gene, have one son and live in Port Huron, Mich.

Penny Kwiat is a dental assistant, homemaker, and pianist who enjoys music, sewing, writing, and taking part in a variety of church activities. She and her husband, Chet, have three children and make their home in Duvall, Wash.

Cecilia Mainord is a homemaker who enjoys crafts, walking, and spending time at the beach. She and her husband, Steve, have two young sons and live in Canyon Country, Calif.

Veronica McNamee is a homemaker who writes articles for newsletters. She enjoys boating, biking, hiking, flower gardening, grandmothering, and volunteering for Love, Inc. She and her husband, Jim, have five grown children and five grandchildren and live in Bellingham, Wash.

Barbra Minar is a writer and speaker who has written several devotions and articles. Author of *Lamper's Meadow* (Crossway), *Close Connections: Creatively Loving Those Nearest You*, and *Unrealistic Expectations: The Thief of a Woman's Joy* (Victor). She and her husband, Gary, have three children and live in Solvang, Calif.

Lois M. Mulnite is a homemaker, part-time office worker, and part-time art teacher. In addition to writing devotions and articles, she enjoys painting, needlework, making dolls, reading, and walking. Lois and her husband have five children and ten grandchildren and live in Broad Brook, Conn.

Joyce Anne Munn is an elementary school teacher who has written numerous devotions and articles for a variety of publications. In addition she enjoys quilting and playing the piano. Joyce makes her home in Watts, Okla.

Geraldine Nicholas has published poems, articles, short stories, devotions, juvenile fiction stories, teaching curriculum, and has been a contributing author to six books. She enjoys reading, decorating, hiking, and crafts. Geraldine has three grown children and lives in Edmonton, Alberta.

Linda Conarty Nylund is a sixth-grade teacher of language arts, reading, and social studies. She is a published writer who enjoys researching Tucson history in preparation for writing a youth fiction series, as well as reading, walking, and hiking. Linda has two daughters and lives in Tucson, Ariz.

Fawn Parish is a writer, speaker, and director of Concerts of Prayer in Ventura County. She has written devotions and is the editor of an interchurch newsletter designed to promote unity and vision in "displaying God's heart to the city." Fawn enjoys kayaking. She and her husband, Joey, have one son and reside in Ventura, Calif.

Margaret Parker is the author of *Unlocking the Power of God's Word* (InterVarsity), *How to Hear the Living Word* (Victor), and several articles. In addition to being a director of women's ministries, she enjoys camping, sewing, and singing. Margaret and her husband, Bill, have one grown daughter and live in Walnut Creek, Calif.

Louise H. Rock is a writer and editor of preschool and primary Sunday School publications for David C. Cook and the Harvester newsletter for Kids Alive International serving children overseas. She enjoys reading, traveling, and snorkeling. She has two foster sons and five foster grandchildren and lives in Valparaiso, Ind.

Alene Adele Roy is a freelance writer and photographer who has over two hundred published articles, poems, stories, and devotions. She enjoys cooking, gardening, photography, and sewing. Alene and her husband, Thomas, have one grown son and live in Scappoose, Ore.

Jessica Shaver is a magazine and newspaper freelance writer. Author of *Gianna: The Girl Who Survived Abortion* (Focus on the Family) and many articles, poems, fillers, and stories, she enjoys reading, photography, and classical music. Jessica and her husband, Rick, have two grown children and reside in Long Beach, Calif.

Marcella Beecher Shaw is a Bible teacher, speaker, and pastor's wife. She has self-published several studies including *The Fragrance of Jesus* and *Girl of My Dreams: A Study of Proverbs 31*. Marcella enjoys music, interior decorating, and traveling. She and her husband have three daughters and four grandchildren and live in Salem, Ore.

Phyllis Shelley privately tutors learning disabled children and teaches piano. She enjoys writing, gardening, and choral music. She has three daughters and one grandson. Phyllis makes her home in Bellingham, Wash.

Judy Slotemaker is a writing instructor, editor, water utility manager, bookseller, and antique dealer. Author of numerous short stories and articles, she enjoys grandmothering, writing, collecting and selling antiques, and traveling. Judy and her husband, Mel, have three children and four grandchildren and live in Lynden, Wash.

Michelle L. Steinbacher is a homemaker and works part time as a register nurse. She enjoys writing and reading. Michelle and her husband, Kurt, have two young sons and make their home in Jersey Shore, Pa.

Dorothy Stephenson is a Bible study leader and active prayer intercessor. Her book *31 Talks with God for the Month of December* is in its third printing. Dorothy enjoys reading, photography, and traveling. She has a son and daughter, two granddaughters, and two grandsons. Dorothy lives in Riverside, Calif.

Betty C. Stevens is the author of several children's stories and articles, as well as two monthly prayer letters for a Christian child care center. Each summer Betty camps with her beagle friend and typewriter for her own spiritual, writing, and walking retreat. She has one daughter and one grandson and lives in Pittsburgh, Pa.

Nancy Witmer is a freelance writer, tour guide, and bookkeeper for a family business. She has written over five hundred articles and devotions, and in 1990 won an Amy Writing Award. Nancy enjoys traveling, camping, and reading. She and her husband, Richard, have two sons and one granddaughter and live in Manheim, Pa.

CREDITS